KING GEORGE

*The Triumphs And
Tragedies In The Life Of
George Strait*

THE KING OF
COUNTRY MUSIC

A Biography By

Austin Teutsch

All Photos Used By Permission From
StraitFever.com
and Courtesy of Linda Robbins.

ISBN: 1456364774

ISBN 13: 978-1456364779

All Other Photos Are By Taylor Teutsch
and Ron Kattner

Golden Touch Press/JRAB L.L.C.
P.O. Box 835
Manchaca, Texas 78652

Contents

"..an amazing story of an amazing life!"

--- Texas Music Magazine

"George Strait…may just be the finest country music performer since Hank Williams."

---Andrew Vaughan
Who's Who In Country Music

"George Strait continues to get better and better."

---Chet Flippo
Billboard Magazine

INTRODUCTION

I first met George Strait in 1970. I was 16 and he was 18. The event was an FFA (Future Farmers Of America) talent show in Cotulla, Texas. I was the drummer for *Charlie Locke And The Country Boys* representing our chapter out of Jourdanton, Texas and George was a member of the Pearsall FFA attending the banquet. We lost the contest to a band ironically from Poteet, Texas, the small town George was born in. I remember him saying he thought we should have won because we had a good lead guitarist. (He's a dentist now in Marble Falls, Texas!)

The next time I ran into George Strait was in 1976 in Pearsall, Texas, his home town just south of San Antonio. I was playing in another country western band at a club out on highway 81 called *The Wishing Well Club*, a converted bowling alley on the edge of town. George had played there the night before and he was helping tear down the band's equipment to head out to another honky-tonk. (Everyone has played at the old Wishing Well Club) George was getting serious about his music, having done two years in the army in Hawaii, having been married to his high school sweetheart, Norma for six years and playing nights while going to college in San Marcos at what was then Southwest Texas State College. (Now it's called Texas State University)

I told him I was gonna head on up to Nashville to work as a studio musician (drummer)and hope to catch on with an up and rising star to tour and see the world. Little did I know I was looking at

This Book Is Dedicated To

JOHNNY BUSH

The Unsung King Of Country Music

And

To all the kings and queens of the country
western dance hall circuit who honky-tonk for
the working men and women of America
every Friday and Saturday nights
across this great land.

YEEHAW!!

the number one up and rising star! He said he wanted to settle down after he graduated from college and take care of his wife and his little girl, Jenifer. His wife had given him one year, ONE year to make it in the music business and that if it didn't work out, he'd get his degree and start teaching agriculture in some high school in South Texas to be near his father's ranch and she near her family in Pearsall. Needless to say, George never taught a class because he made it big the first shot out of the shoot. He became the star we all wanted to be. I admired him because he is the consummate singer and rodeo rider. I'm a country drummer and have ridden a horse since I was 9 years old, so we have a little in common. (I strayed in the 1980's and played in a rock band called Rattlesnake with Brian Wooten, but we both woke up and Brian now is the lead guitar player for Trace Adkins, can't get more conservative country than Trace Adkins)

He wished me well in my dream and I wouldn't see him until 1990. By then George Strait was a huge star, but not too big to play a benefit dance in Round Rock, Texas at the local SPJST hall for an injured rodeo rider he'd known. I mean he didn't just play a few songs and leave, George played a whole two hours for this guy. George had just sold out the Frank Erwin Center in nearby Austin, Texas the night before and the Astrodome in Houston the week before that. A lot had changed in both of our lives by then, both good and bad. I'd been toying with the idea of a biography of George's life for quite some time. We had a lot in common. We both married

7

blondes, we both think "The Outlaw Josey Wales" is the best western ever made, we both grew up in small South Texas towns, we both play country music, we shared the stage at the old Wishing Well Club in Pearsall, Texas we both had two children, we both had great fathers and we both love to ride horses. And, not only because I had known him and met him on a few occasions before he became a big star and I had met many of his family and friends, but because I knew of where he had come from, how he made it and of the highs and lows of his life that only a fellow musician and South Texan could know. Over 35 years, I watched George Strait come from where we all used to live and play music. It was a case of you had to have been there kind of a thing. I was there. I played those same old dance halls, hoping for enough gas money to get back home, dreaming of "making it" in the music business and then when one of our own finally did make it, we believed we actually had a chance, too. When George Strait made it, I cheered him on, proud he beat the odds in a business known for breaking you before making you. I'm sure when he reads this account of his life, he'll be taken back to those early days where the triumphs helped get him through the tragedies that would come his way.

A most remarkable story arose during the research and writing of this book. It seems George's father, John Byron Strait Sr. piddles around the huge ranch George owns in Big Wells, Texas just to stay busy at 88 years old. He lives in Pearsall, Texas, some 30 miles away

8

from Big Wells today as he has done for over 50 years. My son, Taylor went with me to Big Wells to take some pictures and interview some people for this book. At a general store in Big Wells, the only business in town, I asked a lady if she knew where the Big Wells Cemetery was located. She gave me directions and I told her I was working on a book on George Strait.

"Well, you see that man in that truck?" She asked.

"Yeah."

"Well, that's his father."

Taylor and I jumped in the car, only to lose him. Oh, well. Would've made for a good interview. When we got to the cemetery, there was Mr. Strait sitting in his truck in the corner of the cemetery, eating his lunch! I waited for him to finish and then I approached him, introduced myself, told him I was there to take a picture of Buddy's grave for a book I was writing on George. When I told him I was a classmate of Jimmy Tymrak from Jourdanton he chuckled.

"Get in." he said to me with a sly grin. I guess he eats his lunch at the cemetery often because we all know you're not supposed to bury your own children. Parents grieve in their own way when they lose a child. Maybe it's a closeness for him? At 88, he's entitled to do as he pleases no matter how famous his youngest son is. So I got into his brand new Chevy pickup truck and he took me to Buddy's grave. Along the way, we talked about Buddy, George and a few mutual friends, like my old classmate, Jimmy Tymrak, Buddy's old business partner at a oil company they jointly owned called Tasco Tool in Alice, Texas, ironically the small South Texas city my brother and I were born in. He told me Buddy thought the world of Jimmy and I did too. You can't get any better than the Tymrak family from Jourdanton, Texas. I told him I had met Buddy and George over the past 35 years and that my book would be true to the Strait tradition. He liked that. I wasn't trying to butter him up, but I think he saw I was a country boy like his sons and he remembered when my dad had a field office in Big Wells for Dow Chemical Company at the site of an old onion shed in the 1960's. Before I left, my son took the picture of us you see in this book.

"You can take a picture." Mr. Strait said to us. "But I'm not getting out 'cause it takes me too long to get back in!" He just laughed. (I did notice a medical walker in the back seat of his truck.) Mr. Strait reminded me of my late father who was also a hard working man. It's easy to talk to someone who talks straight, no pun intended. The apple really doesn't fall far from the tree. George Strait is a lot like his dad. I'm glad I got the chance to meet him, too. Like George himself says, "There's nothing like getting back down to the ranch in South Texas. It really is God's country. I believe that, too.

So buckle up your spurs, saddle up your horse and let's take a ride down a country road with the King Of Country Music, George Strait.

Austin Teutsch

October, 2010

One
Poteet To Pearsall

Poteet, Texas has always been hot in May, the beginning of summer. The red, juicy red strawberries grown in the sandy soil around the small city have all been picked and sold. Poteet would later become world famous for their crop and their Poteet Strawberry Festival that began in 1948. It would also become famous for the birth of a "King" on May 18th, 1952 when George Harvey Strait was born to Doris Couser Strait and John Byron Strait Sr. He would be the future King Of Country Music and almost single handedly save country music from itself.

In those early days after World War II, small hospitals that were not much more than doctor's clinics with beds opened up in rural Texas towns as the baby boom was in full swing. Dr. John Ogden and Dr. C.C. Shotts (yes, that was his real name) opened up such a hospital in Poteet where George Strait, his older brother John Byron Strait Jr. and his younger sister, Pency were born. Just 22 miles due south of San Antonio, Texas, the hospital was a godsend for those who couldn't make it to the major hospitals up highway 16 to the big city of San Antonio. The Strait family lived in Pleasanton just nine miles from Poteet on Goodwin street in a little yellow house facing Bryant Street, and that was only 9 miles from the only hospital in Atascosa County at the time. A few years later after Mr. Strait acquired the ranch in deep South Texas, they moved to Pearsall.

George joined the Strait family which included his brother, John "Buddy" Strait Jr., who was two years older than George and his younger sister, Pency who came along a couple of years later. Pency was a strange name that was not an abbreviation for any other name, just Pency Strait. Pency Strait became Pency Lieber by an adoption by Paul Lieber when Mrs. Strait married Mr. Lieber after a move to Dallas. Today, Pency is married to Lea Edel and is a school teacher like her blood father, John Strait. She lives in the Dallas suburb of Plano where she is 52 years old and makes a comfortable living teaching at Dooley Elementary for $46,000 per year. It's not known if she has ever asked her multi-millionaire brother George Strait for a loan now and then. Pency Strait Lieber Edel has two step brothers who live in Georgia and New Jersey and two children of her own.

The Strait family would move to nearby Pearsall, Texas in the late fifties as John Strait took a job teaching Jr. High math. He would also acquire a 2000 acre cattle ranch in Big Wells, Texas where his family lived for generations, most are buried in the Big Wells Cemetery dating back to the middle 1800's. As a matter of fact, the most prominent family buried in the Big Wells Cemetery is all Strait with George's ancestors dating back to his great-great grandfather. But there are others that date even farther back.

Coming from German descent on both sides of his family, George is a fourth-great-grandson of Johann Christian Streit (b. 1672) as a native of Kirberg, Bavaria, Germany who migrated to Somerset County, New Jersey before 1710. Within two generations, the family ventured on to Chester County, South Carolina, then onto Greene County, Alabama. The final move was to Texas. His oldest known ancestor was Johannes Streit who was born in 1596 in Bavaria and died in 1664. It seems someone bought brand new tombstones to replace the old ones in the Big Wells Cemetery where many of George's relatives are buried. There are some 10 new markers there today. Can't say for sure, but George probably bought them all when the family placed the headstone for Buddy's grave or when the old ones were so old and worn out you couldn't see the names anymore.

After the move to Texas, to avoid confusion with other Straits that George's ancestors apparently didn't like, they changed the spelling of their name from Streit to Strait. Germans were known to do that. Dietze became Dietz and so on.

Mr. Strait, George's father, worked the ranch running Longhorn cattle to supplement his teacher's pay as a math teacher in Pearsall. Both Buddy and George were in his class when they were in Jr. High. Mr. Strait was one of the most popular teachers in the Pearsall school system. The ranch he owns is in the Texas brush country near the Mexican border. Snakes, dust, cactus and oil wells bathed in blinding heat. San

Antonio to the north and Mexico to the south with not much in between. It's said that in the brush country everything either bites, stings or has thorns. The ranching life would also play an important part in young George's life, both in his choice of music and living a ranching and rodeo existence on the back of horse. He was destined to excel at both. He would become a true Texas cowboy, not one of those drugstore types who only wore their cowboy hats on Saturday nights.

But there was trouble brewing in the Strait family after the move to Pearsall and George entered the third grade. Doris Strait wanted out, the marriage all but over in her mind, a mind that was clinically depressed. That trouble would have a profound effect on young George and his brother, Buddy. Mrs. Strait was depressed all the time. Back in those days, there was very little medicine or treatment to combat such a problem, you either "got over" it or they locked you away. For Doris Strait, she just ran away, left her husband and two young sons and took George's little sister, Pency with her, never to return. It was hard on John Strait Sr. to hold his head up in a small town where divorce was frowned upon. And it wasn't a normal thing either. You were supposed to tough it out, especially if there were small children involved. Divorce was a selfish way out to many of the conservative people of Pearsall, Texas. But John Strait was a well-respected man and teacher. The town accepted the divorce and never once thought ill of Mr. Strait. They knew what happened as does most of small town

America when a citizen has troubles. It's one of the drawbacks of living in rural America where everyone knows everyone's business. You take the good with the bad in those small towns.

With two young boys to raise alone, ages 9 and 11, John Strait remained perplexed as to why a woman would leave the boys so coldly as she did. It wasn't a normal thing. It would be up to him to pull double duty and make life as normal as possible. And Mr. Strait did a good job, not remarrying until the boys were grown and out of the house. He thought of his sons first, and then himself. John Strait is a solid man and that's where George and his brother Buddy got their values. The breakup of the Strait marriage would also serve as a heartbreak for George, one he'd use later on in life through the songs he would sing. His sincere pitch when he sang the songs of the broken heart came from a deep seeded experience. In the world of country music, heartbreak has always been the foundation of its very existence. Paying one's dues through the sad times a musician would have to endure and would almost always come from a loss of some kind. The Strait divorce would be one of the saddest times for George Strait, one he vowed never to repeat should he ever marry...and marry he would!

"He just dedicated his whole life to raising my brother and me." George offered. "He taught school and worked the ranch. It wasn't until Buddy and I got out of the house that Daddy cut loose and started having some fun again and eventually remarry to a wonderful woman named

Anna." George and Buddy were very grateful that their father found someone to share his life with.

Pearsall, Texas was like so many south Texas towns, almost far removed from the rest of the world. Nothing hit Pearsall quickly. Music was no exception. If it was a hot property in New York or Los Angeles, it wouldn't be in Pearsall until many months later. While George was in elementary school, the British invasion hit but Pearsall didn't know about it right away, mainly by the mid-sixties. Back then, there were basically two kinds of music at the time, country and Mexican. You either wore cowboy boots or Stacy Adams shoes, shined to the hilt, no in between. It's also known as the peanut capital of Texas, but it's good for a barrel of oil or two. And you'll see a few head of cattle scattered in the brush along what was once a major railroad stop from the Mexican border to San Antonio. On Independence Day in 1880, Pearsall became a town by selling town lots to folks working the land near the rail line.

In the 1960's the town had a newspaper called the Pearsall Leader which became the Frio Nueces Current newspaper in the 1970's. Named after the two major rivers where George Strait and his high school classmates used to swim and fish, the Frio River was and is indeed, cold. (Frio is cold in Spanish) The Nueces River ran all the way to one of Texas' most beautiful parks, Garner State Park near Uvalde, Texas, the birthplace of Dale Evans, Roy Roger's wife, the King Of The Cowboys. Vice President John Nance Garner was also from Uvalde, which is not far from Pearsall. Garner was vice president under Franklin D. Roosevelt and was famous for the line, "Being vice president isn't worth a bucket of spit."

In the song, "All My Exes Live In Texas" George asked songwriter Whitey Shafer if he could substitute Whitey's river for the Frio River where he really did learn to swim as the words of the song indicate. On the weekends, it was a washtub full of Lone Star Beer and lazy days by those rivers, soaking up the sun, strumming a guitar or listening to the truck's radio or 8-track tapes. Don't remember 8-track tapes? Well, they're hard to find today, even harder than a vinyl record. Don't remember a vinyl record? Well, it was long before CD's and U Tube, that's for sure.

"Go ahead. But don't forget to send the checks!" Shafer added, giving George the change of his lyrics.

Country is the best way to describe Pearsall and the brush country. Oil and peanuts, cattle and vegetables are the main source of income, except if you're a school teacher as George's father was. The pictures in this book indicate every town had a agriculture mascot of sorts. Pearsall was, of course, the peanut. Poteet, where George was born, was home to the strawberry while Crystal City, some 30 miles due west of Pearsall was known for its spinach. Texas is a growers paradise. In the valley, grapefruit and oranges are king. In the hill country outside of Austin, it's peaches and south of San Antonio, it's all about the watermelons and cantaloupes. In Athens, Texas, it's the pecan. Texas is a rich agriculture state for sure and those small farming communities are proud of their crops. So much so, that they erect statues to them instead of dead mayors or councilmen or long ago Governors or Presidents. Go to Philadelphia and you'll see statutes of Ben Franklin and the Liberty Bell. Go to South Texas and you'll see grand statues of the crops produced by those who work the fields and those who profit from that work. Just look at the elaborate statues in the pictures in this book. The small farming communities really do love their crops!

As George entered high school, Pearsall began to catch on to what was called "surfer" music, most of it coming out of California where the Beach Boys sang of catching a wave or catching a beautiful tanned blond. You were either a "surfer" or a "kicker". George started out as a surfer, loving the music of the Beatles and the Beach Boys as he listened to radio station KTSA out of San Antonio with it's ever popular record spinner Bruce Hathaway in the mornings or to Don Couser at KONO before heading back to class. In time, George would punch the radio dial in his worn out truck to radio station KBUC and listen to jockey Ricci Ware play all the country hits out of Nashville with a few locals thrown in such as Adolph Hofner And The Pearl Wranglers or Paul And Juanita Thompson. Of course before the corporate play list of today's radio station where if you were a local act, you'd never get any airtime. George had many Mexican friends, too. He wasn't above listening to Conjunto or what would later become, Tejano music. Later on in his musical career, George would record a song entirely in Spanish and some of his biggest hits have been influenced by Mexican chord progressions. You couldn't live in Pearsall or South Texas for that matter without being influenced by the Mexican culture and the music behind it. And what a great culture it is.

There were two sets of whites ("gringos") back in those early days in Pearsall and the surrounding towns like it where there was a large Mexican and Mexican-American population. Some whites embraced their Mexican friends, and some resented them as they're beginning to do today with the immigration problem and drug traffic that's going down. George was one of the gringos who had many Mexican friends and would come to their aid whenever the other side began a racist slur or action. In those days while working side by side, some gringos still believed in the old adage that "black may be beautiful, tan is grand, but white is the color of the big boss man." Just as the blacks and the whites of the deep south had their racial problems, so did South Texas. Not enough has been written or explored about those early days when those crops had to be brought in for all of America. But George Strait had no problem with it. He was a friend to anyone who worked as hard as he did. And you can't work a ranch without working hard. Cattle don't feed themselves and fences don't mend on their own. It was the Mexican worker who worked alongside the white establishment who built South Texas into what it was and what it is today. Period. Don't be fooled by those in Washington. Hard work is not what Washington is all about unless they grab a sack and pick the lettuce, the onion or the watermelon. In Pearsall and those surrounding towns that were born and bred from that kind of hard work is what made this country great. And it's also what made the men and women who worked it great. The Strait family was part of that hard work.

In high school, there was tension between the races of tan and white. But George used his music to soothe it all out the best he could. In the early 1970's, many Mexican-Americans were embracing country music as they all went to school together, tan and white, and they all listened to the same radio stations out of San Antonio and Laredo. But, it was students like George Strait who helped ease those racial tensions as he had so many Mexican-American friends, both in school and out on the ranch. With the climate of immigration today, it's getting harder to work those ranches with hands that don't have documentation to be in the United States. Pearsall was no different from many of the small farming and ranching communities who depended on Mexican labor to get the job done. Washington had better get the job done and set up some kind of immigration workforce idea so that the crops can be picked, the beds made in the hotels and the oil grabbed from the ground. It's very basic.

George had to make a decision while a freshman at Pearsall High School in 1967. Should he stay in band and play the trumpet? Should he join the football team or should he just stick with the guitar? While many of his classmates such as Danny Hubba and Paul Pitts played football, George decided to become a solid guitar player to back up his singing. He knew early on he had a pretty good voice. His classmates seemed to like it when he'd play at parties and BBQ's. So the choice was easy and led by his desire to become a country music singer. In those days, if you had an ounce of talent, you could lead a band. If you had a pound of talent like George did, you could make money singing and playing. Why? Because there really weren't that many good bands out there in those days. In Atascosa and Frio counties back in George's growing up years there were only six bands from the local area who were good enough to make money at playing country western dances. And, those bands were always competing with bands from San Antonio where the musicians were studio ready. Steel guitar players like Bubba Overstreet and guitar players like Garland Arnold or drummers like Debby Davis. Man, these cats could have been working in Nashville studios instead of worn out dance halls. They were some of the finest country music players in the nation working those old clubs and dance halls.

While George was working those same dance halls, there were real country stars in the making who you knew were going to make it big. In

South Texas, there was a young lady in the 1960's named Billie Wright who was the true country western singer. She had the voice of an angel and could play the acoustic guitar better than most men. She was a throwback to the old days of Patsy Montana and Wanda Jackson, both who are true legends of country music today. Unlike George Strait, Billie was married to a jealous man who wanted her at home, rattling those pots and pans and taking care of babies and such. She never made it, although she could've been the George Strait of South Texas, a national talent like George. Again a sign of the times.

George was still trying to find his own place while in high school in Pearsall, Texas. While going to dances that featured singers like Billie Wright and other South Texas up and comers, George was between what he wanted to do and what the others in his age group were doing, like playing sports or playing in the band.

"About the time most young men were playing Little League baseball, I was learning how to rope and ride and play the guitar." George said. "I knew that's what I wanted to do with my life."

In those days, you made your decision and stuck with it. Not like today where most kids don't know what they want to do. Most want to do what they do in front of a computer screen. In those early days of playing music, your desire and your time was spent on chasing the dream, a dream that was laid out by those four guys from Liverpool, England. Didn't matter if you were country or not back then, you wanted that same kind of fame and adulation. Those guys had it and you wanted it.

George was captivated by the Beatles as most teens were in the sixties. Especially musicians. While learning to play guitar and how to sing, he would play Beatle tunes or Beach Boy songs and the songs of the other major acts of the day in small bands in and around Pearsall. Even though George had a very fine voice, his vocal range was limited. When any musician saw The Beatles on the old Ed Sullivan Show out of New York City, that's what they wanted to be, musically. George had that twang, that smooth country register that begged him to sing country and western music. Since very few could sing like Paul McCartney or Brian Wilson, George knew where he had to go. And in South Texas at the time, there were a lot more "kickers" than there were "surfers". Country was where the money was at. Only in the 1970's did you see bands such as Wheatstraw out of Victoria or The Kustoms out of Goliad began to play "mixed sets" with country and western and rock and roll in the same dances. In those old small dance halls of South Texas, horns and organs began to show up. The only time you saw a horn back in those days was when you saw a conjunto band or a German polka band. It was rare. When rock and roll began to share the stage with country, then came the horns and other the instrumentation of rock era. And, then came the long hair!

The long hair was the main point of contention for many schools and the country western music lover. Many a dance hall fight began because of a guy's long hair. Why? Because the girls were beginning to fall for guys with long hair. In the 1970's, with Willie Nelson growing his hair out, other country acts of the "outlaw" movement followed right along with old Willie. But George Strait never did. He remained as country as he is today.

By the time George was getting interested in country music and learning to play the guitar at the age of 15, he was also getting interested in girls. In small town Texas, the pickings were always slim for the cream of the crop, so to speak. Even though George was a handsome boy when he was in elementary school, he had some dental issues and he wasn't very tall. Even today, with his teeth fixed to perfection, his height stopped at 5'10". Nothing anyone could do about that, though. A lot of kids in the post war era of the fifties had braces because the economy was thriving and parents had extra money to pay for braces on a monthly basis. Amazing that a set of braces in the late sixties and early seventies only cost $400 dollars. But then gas was 42 cents a gallon while milk was 35 cents a gallon. Oh, for the good old days!

Obviously, George's height wasn't too much of a problem for girls in Frio County as they looked at George with approval. He was a popular boy by the time he got to high school and his growing ability to sing and play only added fuel to the fire the girls would have for him.. Musicians always attract girls no matter how tall they are. If Keith Richards and Mick

Jagger of the Rolling Stones can get a girl, anyone can get a girl. And there were so many guys and girls who thought they had a voice or the talent to play music, but they didn't. They were usually the kids of the rich who bought them the best Fender equipment and the P.A systems and told them how great they were when they couldn't carry a tune in a paper bag. George saw it time and time again. He just had his old guitar and a small amp and made his way to the stage with what he had, like most country musicians did. Oh, those rich musicians whose parents thought they'd be the next Beatles? Well, they're the insurance agents and lawyers and doctors and such today. And, that's the truth!

The first full-fledged country music star from South Texas would emerge from Sabinal, Texas, a very small town not far from Pearsall and just due East of San Antonio. There were acts such as Willie Nelson and Hank Thompson and His Brazos Valley Boys from up above Central Texas who had gone to Nashville to "make it" in the music business, but that's not South Texas. As a matter of fact, no one from South Texas had ever made it big before a Mexican boy named Johnny Rodriquez burst on the scene.

Rodriquez would hit Nashville hard with hits such as "Pass Me By" and "Jealous Heart" in the early seventies. Women threw their panties and bras at him the same way they'd thrown them at Elvis years before. He was a handsome boy and had a smooth voice as he toured the small towns of Texas to support his rising popularity. George took in one of Johnny's early shows when Johnny was touring with 12 year old Tanya Tucker and decided that country music was better than rock and roll. Without a doubt, Johnny was getting rich and famous *and* getting all the girls to boot! Never mind the Beatles or the Beach Boys. Playing country music seemed easier and more attainable for George and it would be a wise choice to follow the road that Johnny Rodriquez had forged. With his guitar in hand, George Strait would began his rise to stardom by playing the songs of Johnny Bush, Lefty Frizzell, Merle Haggard, Charlie Pride and Buck Owens. The music of the world had finally made its way to Pearsall, Texas and when it did, George Strait made his choice to do it country style.

When Nashville accepted Johnny Rodriquez as a solid country music star, they played up the story of his being discovered singing in Uvalde jail cell after stealing a goat in Garner State Park. The truth is the goat was stolen, but not by Johnny. He was just sitting by the fire playing his old beat up guitar as the party's entertainment as the goat was being BBQ and the entire party went down to the Uvalde County Jail for the theft. No, Johnny got his start playing shows at Happy Shahan's Alamo Village in Bracketville, Texas where the original John Wayne movie "The Alamo" was filmed in 1960. That's where Tom T. Hall found him after a Texas Ranger named Joaquin Jackson heard him singing and told Hall about him. That's when Hall brought Johnny to Nashville to play rhythm guitar in his band, "The Storytellers."

Whenever a small Texas town had a festival in the late 60's and early 70's, they would usually hire a major musical act to play the Saturday night dance. Those dances were almost always held right in the street under the stars in the sky. A small city near Pearsall called Pleasanton held their annual Cowboy Homecoming, a big celebration of eating, drinking, roping and riding flavored with country western music. With the emergence of Tejano music, the city began to bring in huge acts such as David Lee Garza based in nearby Poteet. Pleasanton would hire a big time act of the day such as Ray Price or Johnny Paycheck or Gary Stewart as the headliner. George Strait would draw his stage presence from those early live shows passing through town. It was a controversial time in country music where the hard core acts were fighting for air time with the newly organized pop country acts such as Chrystal Gayle. Even Debbie Boone and Marie Osmond were going quasi-country with stringed arrangements. But the excitement of any major star coming to a small South Texas town was an event not soon forgotten. Later on, George Strait would "open" up shows by those stars like Price and the local stars such as Moe Bandy or Darrel McCall as they passed through town. Big regional acts such as the Texas Top Hands shared the stage with George and his Ace In The Hole Band after George began to get a name himself. Working those one-nighters was hard work, but it was paying dues as all the bands who have ever made had to do. Those other acts such as Bubba Littral, Darrell McCall and Moe Bandy from San Antonio, Joe Stampley from Springhill, Louisiana, and Dotsy from Seguin, Texas would play a Saturday night dance while George and his band would play the Friday night gig. Back then, George wasn't a star, just a singer in the band. A very good dance band. Although he was the focus of the Ace In The Hole Band back then, it was the band itself that was the draw. It would take a Nashville A&R man to decide if George should be brought to the forefront, if he was the star of the band. And that would come later on as George's ability began to shine through.

George was influenced by the old school country singers of yesteryear. Ernest Tubb, Floyd Tillman and Lefty Frizzell who remained true to country music and the harsh reality of life as it was lived by real people. Then George Jones and Merle Haggard took the baton and ran with it. Today, George Strait and performers such as Clint Black and Randy Travis carry on the true country tradition. Those who think George Jones is the greatest country singer of all time are now saying George Strait is. Though, it's hard to argue with either. Both George's have come to country music's rescue. George Jones along with the late great Buck Owens saved country music in 1966 when the strings of Patsy Cline and Jim Reeves tried to redefine it at it's very core. That's not taking a thing from those two legends of country music because they were in fact, playing country music. But the producers of country music have always been at the heart of the problem, influenced by the recording studios of New York and Los Angeles. They are constantly telling new acts to add this or take this out because you want a bigger audience. George Jones and George Strait have held steadfast to the true roots of country music and from time to time, they have to cut a song to bring country music back in line.

George Jones hit the country music scene in the early sixties and had that special twang that George Strait has, even though Jones' is more of a backwoods country sound while George Strait has a smooth, baritone delivery. Both are pure country, one a little more citified than the other. It's up the listener to determine which is which! Jones had a hit with a song that has been called the greatest country music song ever recorded. Jones' "He Stopped Loving Her Today" is indeed a great country song, maybe one of the top five ever recorded. But Jones' ex-wife, Tammy Wynette has recorded what is perhaps the best known country song of all time when she went into the studio with the great Epic producer Billy Sherill and cut "Stand By Your Man."

But when you look at the field of great country songs, George Strait will come to hold the record for not only the most number ones, but singing some of the best known country songs of the past 25 years. It's hard to overlook George Strait's multi-million sellers that are staples of radio airplay in today's market place.

There were some very good bands back then when George was honing his craft. Al Dean and the All Stars were a top band as was Adolph Hofner and the Pearl Wranglers out of San Antonio, sponsored by Pearl Beer. The old Hofner band bus is now parked in the parking lot of James White's Broken Spoke in Austin, Texas on South Lamar Boulevard. Go by to see it when you're in Austin because that old bus tells the story of the early days of country music bands that played in Texas in the 1940's and 50's.

The Farmer's Daughter in San Antonio was one of the best known clubs where Patsy Cline, Ernest Tubb and Bob Wills all played on the raised bandstand. George and his Ace In The Hole Band would play there and clubs such as New Braunfels' Chrystal Chandelier or San Marcos' Cheyenne Social Club with it's uneven wooden dance floor primed for a shot of corn meal to smooth out the dancer's two-step.

One of the saddest things about playing and singing back in those early days was that there wasn't room for everybody to be a star. Just look at today's corporate play lists at today's radio stations. In Jourdanton, there was a boy just as good as George Strait and George himself will agree. His name was David Riley and together with his Western Hearts, he was a solid draw night after night. One night at the Poteet Strawberry festival, David drew close to 3,000 people! Singing much like George Jones with a powerful whine that was pure country, Riley never made it. The son of a Pentecostal Preacher, Riley could belt out a song as if he was dying right there on the stage. Many a night, dancers would stop in their tracts just to watch this guy pour his heart out in the song he was singing. George Strait had that same affect on his crowd. His delivery wasn't as forceful as Riley's, but the smoothness of his voice, his technical ability and intonation made George Strait a startling singer, one that hadn't come along in quite some time. George's success today is a combination of talent, luck, timing and having the total package with handsome looks to seal the deal. Every once and a while a singer makes it by not being the "total package". But why a David Riley didn't make it and George Strait did is because one of those elements was missing. Riley was handsome and wiry and super talented, but he didn't catch the breaks that George Strait did. But that's show business, and it is a business, never forget it.

George Strait caught the breaks along the way. If it hadn't been for Erv Woolsey and Kent Finlay and his time on stage in San Marcos while in college, George may have fallen by the wayside as did a David Riley. But the breaks did come his way and he was talented and smart enough to take advantage of them. Johnny Rodriquez did the same thing before George Strait. But Johnny couldn't handle fame and fortune. Today, he still performs but a drug habit and drinking have taken away much of what he was. And, killing that guy in Sabinal in the late 1990's didn't help his image much either. Talk about living out the words of your songs! George Strait may sing of lost love, drunken nights and the other woman, but he doesn't live that kind of life and never has.

But it wasn't until George entered Pearsall High School that he really began to think he could play music for money. He didn't play football. But he did play trumpet in the fighting Pearsall Maverick band. So did his brother, Buddy. In time, he put that aside to concentrate on playing guitar. It's well known that it's more fun to ride on the band bus with the twirlers and cheerleaders than on the football bus with a bunch of hairy legged old boys! George wasn't dumb by any means.

George had been riding a horse since he was a little boy. As good as he is as a singer, he's even a better rodeo rider, if that can be believed. But, it's true. He'd learn to ride and rope on his daddy's ranch in Big Wells and thought he might become a rodeo star like Larry Mahan or Phil Lyne from nearby West, Texas. If he hadn't made it big as a singer, there is little doubt George Strait would have been a rodeo star. Rodeos were and are big in Texas. In the 1960's, Texas held its annual Texas Prison Rodeo in Huntsville, Texas and it was one of the biggest and most dangerous rodeos in the country. The prisoners did the riding and roping and they didn't care if they got hurt. What's to lose when you're doing life without parole? Lots of broken legs and arms and an occasional death. But, the do good citizens came calling with their politically correct banners and the prison rodeo is no more. Buddy Strait was also roping and riding and even playing a little guitar. Some say he was as good as his brother George.

George was trying to do both, play and ride. Buddy said there was no reason a man couldn't do both. Roy Rogers never had to give up his horse or his guitar! To this day, George does both equally well, playing and singing and roping and riding. He really is a cowboy troubadour.

In those early days of playing dance halls in South Texas, a boy of 15 or 16 could play music, drink beer, chase girls from the pick of the litter and make a few bucks doing it. George did it before Norma caught his eye. And a few of the bands he'd play in would play for the door, which meant they'd be paid by whoever showed up to dance. Some nights, it was a good payday, enough gas money to get back home with a little extra for the coming week. Some nights, it was hell to pay, not enough money to buy a McDonalds hamburger at 25 cents a pop. (Remember when you could buy a McDonalds hamburger for that price?)

Pearsall was country. The town made it's mark for peanuts, but when George was finishing up high school, the town had another oil boom going on. And the workers were wild at the dances he'd play. There was an old bar in Los Angeles, Texas, (yes there is a Los Angeles, Texas) called Ruby's. It was out in the middle of nowhere, literally. An oil field crew was drinking there one night and old Ruby told them "times up, boys" got to go. They didn't want to leave. When she threatened to call the Sheriff, they got in their crew cab company truck and drove it through the front door an out the back door! And at the old Red Dog Lounge in Freer, Texas, they put up chicken wire to protect the band from flying bottles just like in the movie "The Blues Brothers." Those are the kinds of dance halls George played in those early days when the oil flows, so does the beer. When the beer flows, so does the rowdiness. But you were playing to make money and get your name out there it really didn't matter much. You stuck it out and played the dance. In those days, you usually played from 9 until 1 and averaged thirty bucks a man. Not a bad pay for the early seventies. And there were nights where you hit the jackpot and played for the door at two bucks a head. When 100 heads came through the door, an average band of four made fifty bucks each! Now you're talking. Do that three times a week and you're a professional musician making enough money to actually live on.

One such dance had all the makings of a bomb. George was 17 and fronting a band he'd booked himself into an old barn in Cotulla, Texas. He'd promised to pay the band out of his own pocket if no one showed up at the door. It was a cold Christmas Eve night and by 10 p.m. only a few heads had come through the door. It looked bad. And George was sweating it, having only a few bucks himself to live up to his word. As talent hooked up with a little bit of luck, by 11 p.m. the barn was packed to the rafters with farmers, ranch hands, oil field workers and everyone else. Each of the five members of the band made $67.00 that night. A virtual goldmine had been found! George Strait was well on his way to packing them in as fans were starting to take notice of this boy from the neighborhood. And George himself began to feel singing country music was his ticket to stardom. But America was at war in 1968 and Uncle Sam put a target on boys like George Strait.

Dances such as the Christmas Eve dance would be the basis for George's desire to not only play country music, but to learn how to make a living at it, the business end of making it big. It would serve him well when he would one day go to Nashville a decade later and dive into that snake pit where cutthroat players come in all shapes and sizes. Showcasing one's talents is one thing. Taking care of business is another. Just ask anyone who's been screwed while trying their hand at both. It has been said that a record executive is just one step below a used mobile home salesman. George would learn that early on and excel at both showcasing himself and taking care of his business because he had a good head on his shoulders and always kept it simple. Never cloud the issue as that only gives the other side an avenue to take you to the cleaners.

And just like Johnny Rodriquez before him, George Strait would become the next star to make it from South Texas, a place far behind the times because that's the way they like it and where any kind of star is still high up in the wide Texas sky.

Two
Mexico

When George was 17, he met the love of his life when he saw Norma Voss twirling a baton in band. She was 15 and the girl next door. Pretty with long blond hair, Norma had more than a few lined up to take her hand along with her equally pretty sister, Barbara Voss. They were both twirlers in the band and George was smitten by her strong independence and flirting manner. Norma thought the same of George. She was so in love by the time they starting dating seriously that she wanted George to marry her. They fell in love together at the same time and became inseparable. If you saw George, you saw Norma. It was the classic high school love affair that blossomed into a love that holds firm some 40 years later.

After George graduated with honors from Pearsall High School, he headed to San Marcos, Texas to attend Southwest Texas State University. The University included alumni such as former President Lyndon Johnson and actor Powers Boothe. It changed its name in the early part of the 2000's to Texas State University. But it's still home to the Bobcats.

George and Norma were so head over heels in love, spending time together all the time, they couldn't stand to be apart. So much so, that George couldn't live without her and neither could she. He left college, gathered her up before anyone else could move in on her and took her to Nuevo Laredo, Mexico and eloped!

Mexico always had a romantic lure for South Texas boys. What the Chicken Ranch was to Texas A&M cadets, Mexico was to any boy living south of San Antonio. It had a whorehouse called Boys Town and a sleazy little square of row houses called Papa Gayos where for 10 bucks you could...well, you get the picture. But, that wasn't what George Strait and Norma Voss were up to. They were the classic couple in love and they knew Mr. John Strait and Norma's parents wouldn't go for their children getting married at such a young age. But they did in Mexico where no one questioned one's age or why they were getting married. Back then, along the Mexican border, there were small churches and cottages much like they have in Las Vegas today for young couples to wed in secrecy.

When the newlyweds got back to Pearsall and told everyone what they had done, the anger subsided and all the parents conceded that they should have a proper wedding in the proper way. It was decided that since the couple had already gotten married and were headstrong about it, it might be a good Idea to let them lead their own lives the way they wanted to. It was a time of rebellion, a time of the free spirit and free love and letting it all hang out. George and Norma came home and had that traditional church wedding on December 4th, 1971. The dust had settled and the young couple would embark on a love that still lasts to this day some 40 years later. They celebrated their 39th wedding anniversary in 2010. As one of George's songs says, they "must be doing something right."

George knew he couldn't leave such a pretty girl alone in Pearsall with all the tomcats running loose. So he put that wedding ring on her finger before he went back to college after their time in Hawaii while he was in the army. The pickings were still pretty slim and he knew someone would snatch her up if he didn't take care of business. But college would have to wait as Vietnam was at full throttle. It was a scary situation for boys George's age. Boys were dying and Pearsall, Texas had its share of young men going over there to fight in a most controversial war. Strange how history repeats itself as we see war in the Middle East that doesn't look like it will end anytime soon.

So George decided that before he was drafted by Uncle Sam, he'd join up. After boot camp, George caught the break of a lifetime. He was stationed at the Scofield Barracks in Hawaii and became a member of the 25th Infantry Division. Norma went with him and finished her schooling there. George also caught the next big break when he was asked by a country music fan who was a General and base commander to front a band to entertain all the troops on base. George hardly ever wore the drab green uniform of the Army. He was allowed to wear his civilian clothes and never had to pull guard duty or KP duty in the kitchen. He had a smooth ride in a land where the sun almost always shined on the sandy beaches of the Pacific Ocean.

The marriage that began in a little church in Mexico was now a solid union in beautiful Hawaii, a virtual two year army stint turned into a two year honeymoon for George and Norma Strait. Within a few months of living there, Norma became pregnant with their first child. With a child on the way, George wanted to make more money than the scant pay the army provided. He would play clubs in and around the barracks to supplement his young family. In between playing the NCO club on base, he joined a band called "Santee" which George renamed "Rambling Country". It was sponsored by the army as goodwill and entertainment for the boys who were training to head out should the war effort call them.

After the move to Hawaii on October 6th, 1971, a bright light would shine in George and Norma's marriage in the form of a beautiful baby girl they named Jenifer. To make sure she was as strong and independent as her mother, they purposely left out one "n" in her name. Most parents who name their daughter Jenifer spell it Jennifer. Jenifer would grow up to be an equally beautiful young teenager in Texas when George's army stint was completed in 1975. He was honorably discharged and the young family moved back to San Marcos, Texas where George would once again enroll at Southwest Texas State University. He would finally get that degree in agriculture education in 1979 but he would never really use it as a bread winner. Changes were on the horizon for George Strait. Some good and some very, very bad. 1981 would be one of the best years of his life. 1986 would be a nightmare.

To keep food on the table, George worked in between classes in a little town near San Marcos called Martindale where he worked on a ranch mending fences and feeding cattle. He was also playing in bars to keep his chops up and make a few extra bucks doing it. Although money was tight, the young family made due with whatever money came in.

George played in various bands, but it was his good looks, his rich voice and his easy going ways that proved to be the drawing card. One of the first bands he fronted was called "Stoney Ridge". He found them off a calling card posted at the University's library as the band was looking for a singer and guitar picker. They played San Marcos Cheatham Street Warehouse, Gruene Hall in nearby New Braunfels, Texas and the famous Farmer's Daughter down the road in San Antonio. The Cheatham Street Warehouse dances would prove to be George's ticket to stardom. Stoney Ridge was the beginning of George's now famous Ace In The Hole Band as they played their first gig at Cheatham Street Warehouse on October 15th 1975. They also played at a bar called The Prairie Rose. It would be between those two bars that George would meet the man who would pave the way for his 30 year plus career, Erv Woolsey.

"When I first heard George sing," Woolsey said, "I was standing in the back of the club with my back to him. When I heard him crank it up, I just had to turn around to see who was singing.

Right then I knew he was something really special."

Woolsey was from Houston, Texas and had been working radio promotion for Decca records and a few other companies in the late sixties and early seventies. He sold the bar and went to Nashville to head up country music promotion for MCA Records. George and Erv would begin a professional relationship as Erv became George's manager, a position he still holds today. No one gets to George Strait unless they talk to Erv Woolsey first. That's one thing about George Strait, he has always lived up to his name, straight down the line. Having learned from his parent's divorce, relationships mean a lot to George Strait and he cherished them. He knew that in order to make them last, you had to work at it, make a personal effort to keep them. Never give up on the ones who brought you to the dance was George's way of dealing with people. And keep it simple always.

During those early days on the stage, George and his band shared time with other bands of the day. Johnny Bush and the Bandaleros was a real influence on George Strait as he wanted to be a true country western singer like Bush, real down home honky-tonk singing and playing. Johnny Bush was the real deal to George. So was the legendary Ray Price. Even today when you see the 84 year old Price sing, you just get goosebumps all over, a true star. With South Texas bands such as the Kustoms out of Goliad, Texas, The Jess DeMaine Band of Austin and The Debonairs out of Taylor and the late great

Billy Wayne Blankenship and the Melody Mustangs out of Pleasanton, Texas, George shared the stage with some real dues paying hard core country acts. In time, he would get bigger shows backing up bands like the Texas Playboys and the Texas Top Hands and travel as far away as Huntsville, Texas and on into Houston, then down to Corpus Christi. Stoney Ridge was the beginning of a professional musical career for George. Even today, most of those early pickers are still with George in the form of his Ace In The Hole Band, the band he uses on the road. Man, they are hot and get a standing ovation themselves where ever they go with George. Terry Hale, the bass player and Mike Daily, the steel guitarist were former classmates of Georges' in college at the ole Southwest Texas State University in San Marcos, Texas.

Like almost all college towns, there were plenty of bars since back then as the drinking age was 18. George played 'em all. But playing those small clubs would end when Erv cornered a friend of his at MCA records and told him to come down to Texas and take a look at this Strait kid. The MCA representative came down to one of George's shows at Kent Finlay's Cheatham Street Warehouse in San Marcos, Texas and signed him on the spot. In the 1980's, country western music was having an identity crisis. It would be acts like George Strait, Clint Black and Randy Travis who would save country music from itself. The Hammond B-3 organs, the horns and the violins from pop flavored country music of the 1970's such as Crystal Gayle and Olivia Newton-John had to be arrested and let country music get back to its roots. Bob Wills and Hank Williams, those kinds of acts was what was needed. These so called "Hat Acts" did in fact come just in the nick of time. But it was George Strait who stayed more true to country music than the others, leaving the flying over audiences in the arenas to Brooks and the acting on television to Travis. He was a dance hall troubadour and still is to this day, although the dance halls have gotten noticeably bigger.

As George took to those early dance halls, he worked at ranching but he wouldn't do it for long. At least not for a lively hood. MCA had big plans for George Strait. They saw him as the star, not the rest of the Ace In The Hole Band. They threw a pot load of money at him to be the front man, the star and knew the rest of the band was just a band to them. In reality, bass players, guitar players and drummers are a dime a dozen in Nashville, good ones, too. They're everywhere, washing dishes, waiting tables and selling used cars. But to be a star, to be the focus of the band, you had to be a good singer, too. George Strait fit the bill for MCA.

MCA came calling and George answered. Norma told George she'd give him one year, one year to "make it" in the music business, then they'd have another child. She was proud that George finished with his degree in agriculture education to have some solid income because the music business was never rock solid. You never knew when you're going to be a has been.

Norma Strait was an even keeled woman. It's one of the things that has kept George lined up. It is true that behind every great man is a great woman.

George flew to Nashville when MCA called him in 1980. MCA is a solid label, having country and rock and roll divisions with many of the top stars of the day on their rosters. George would cut a demo tape and the producers would try to find him a single. The one thing that has kept George Strait on top from the very beginning was his uncanny ability to pick a hit song. Even though he tried to write songs early on and had a couple of them recorded in Houston on the "D" label, it was his sixth sense at picking out a song that matched his vocal style. He's been right 57 times in 30 years! Not a bad track record. As a matter of fact, it IS the record today and may never be broken.

"I remember I was washing my car and I had these two little boxer puppies at my feet the first time I heard "Unwound" on the car radio." George said. "It was a real thrill and I knew I was on the right track."

In 1980, George came back home to San Marcos with stars in his eyes. He cut the song "Unwound" and the folks at MCA liked what they heard. George didn't know or couldn't have known that "Unwound" would be the beginning of his wealth and fame. He would never use that agriculture degree to teach, although it helped in running his 20 thousand acre ranch and the other ranches and properties he would come to own. And he would never toil again for his bread and butter, although he loved to work the ranch right beside his ranch hands, getting his hands dirty and his back wet with sweat. They say few last in the world of entertainment. Some burn out. Some fall out. And some just peter out. George Strait's ride to the top is on a trail without an end because of the man he is. There were bumps along the way, but really there haven't been all that many in his musical career. In fact, he and Norma have lived virtually on easy street since 1980 when he came back a millionaire from Nashville. And George earned it as he really is the total package. He's just a darn good man.

But, when the lows came, they came hard, as hard as they can ever get for a young couple coping with stardom, riches and fame. No amount of money could ever ease the pain of what was on the horizon for George and Norma Strait. The hits kept coming from 1981 to 1986 musically but they would take the biggest hit of all in 1986, one that would crush their world and make being a star seem like a burned out cinder.

Three
Hawaii

While stationed in Hawaii, George and Norma were on a virtual vacation. The islands are beautiful. Many people take their yearly vacations there and a lot have their honeymoon there. This was back before Americans found Cancun and Belize. But it takes quite a lot of money to live there. A young couple living on a army's pay with a few bucks here and there from playing clubs barely makes the living easier. When a hamburger costs $2.75 in 1974 in Hawaii, you eat a lot of macaroni and cheese or the old standby, PB&J.

"I started getting interested in country music my senior year of high school." George said recently in an interview with Country Weekly magazine. "I always knew I wanted to be a singer, but it wasn't until I ended up in Hawaii that I really got serious about it."

While in Hawaii, George bought a six string guitar, a Hank Williams songbook and sheet music by George Jones and Merle Haggard and taught himself to play guitar like a professional musician. He would sit around the supply room, strumming his guitar and teaching himself to master the art of a guitar singer. When he caught that lucky break from the General who decided to form the country band to entertain the troops after George had auditioned for him, he honed his musical skills for the remaining two years of his stint which would be the foundation of his musical future. George learned how to perform in front of an audience in Hawaii, getting comfortable with the stage. The band played at many parties and official functions. Charles Hargett and Walt Peters were in that army band which was called "Ramblin' Country." Peters is credited with bringing George on board when the army decided to put a band together to entertain the troops. George made good use of that time as an army musician.

"It gave me the time I needed to learn all about playing dates, because it's, you know, a scary thing to do that at first." He added.

In 1974, the Straits decided to try to live in Hawaii and did for six months after George's tour was up in the army. But, the cost of living was just too high and in 1975, they returned to Texas. One of the things George took with him from Hawaii was the G.I. Bill which he would use to pay for his education. He would also come back to Texas as a professional country western singer and performer. The time in Hawaii was well spent getting his style down pat and when he hit Texas soil, he was ready to make a run for fame and fortune.

But Norma wanted him to get his education first. So did his father. The older generation knew you have to have an education or at least a skill to fall back on should things go sour. Mr. Strait, like most fathers of musicians, worried when the day would come that George would have to go out and get a "real" job. Being a professional singer was not considered a "real" job, especially by hard working men like John

Strait. She wanted to one day have another baby and she was worried about the music business as well she should be. Not all the days of being a professional musician could be sunny days like Hawaii. She was worried when the clouds might roll in. There were a lot of singers out there who lived high on the hog only to be one-hit wonders. It could've happen to George. "Unwound" could have been his one and only hit. We all know now that it didn't turn out that way, but Norma was very practical. So was George. He had seen a few come and go in the music business, some who touched stardom and faded away. Where are they now? Who knows. Maybe back to waiting tables on music city row. But it is well known that George Strait used that time in the army in Hawaii to become more that a one hit wonder. We all know where he is today and how he got to the top. And thanks to a General who saw something in George that Erv Woolsey and millions of others still see today, George Strait has become one of the greatest country singers of all time. And the time in Hawaii was a big part of how George was able to get that way. You gotta start somewhere and know when the timing is right. The time in Hawaii was the right time and place for George to make a final decision to play country music forever. Oh, he'd finish college to appease his wife and father, but the things he learned while getting it down in Hawaii would be the basis for where he is today. He probably knew by the reception he was getting in Hawaii that he was destined to be a country music singer, maybe a country music star! Now we know, right?

When you're in the army, anything that remotely seems like home is a welcomed sight. Music brings a lonely sailor or cadet a little bit of home. George played die-hard country music in Hawaii and the troops really liked him. Their reception helped George in his stage presence. They were all in the same boat, not knowing if they'd be deployed to fight in the Vietnam war. George really didn't know either. His easy job of being a clerk and playing for the brass wasn't etched in stone. Should the war escalate, you went where you were told. For the years George was in the army in Hawaii, he lucked out and never saw combat. And, there's nothing wrong with that. No kid wants to get shot at thousands of miles from home.

The high prices in Hawaii sent the Straits packing to San Marcos, Texas and they left the beautiful islands behind them. With their little girl in tow and his army time over, George came back to the mainland to start a new life, a different life, a wonderful life. The future looked bright for the young Strait family. By the time they got to Texas, the war was winding down. George would look on his time in the army as doing the right thing serving his country as many movie stars did during World War II. He wasn't a star, yet. But after the move back to Texas, he was well on his way.

Four
San Marcos

San Marcos, Texas is a college town nestled in the hills of the rock formation called the Balconies Fault zone just off interstate 35 between San Antonio and Austin. Alumni include former President Lyndon Johnson and actor Powers Boothe as stated. In fact, President Johnson, after graduating from what was then Southwest Teacher's College before becoming Southwest Texas State University, wound up in George's neck of the woods when he taught school in Cotulla, Texas, the small city 30 miles south of Pearsall where George grew up. The President taught with a lady named Opal Brooks who wound up in Jourdanton, Texas and taught school there for many, many years. Quite a circle of history there.

In the 1970's, San Marcos, Texas was also a tourist town with Wonder Cave and Aquarena Springs amusement park with its glass bottom boats, it's underwater mermaid shows, it's sky rail and a small zoo. The San Marcos river runs right through it and Ali McGraw and Steve McQueen frolicked in it in 1972 during the filming of "The Getaway". It's a beautiful river with a tube shoot coming out of what was once an old ice house. It's the perfect place to go to college. Some say Southwest Texas State University is a party school, and it is with students stripping and drinking in the sunlight by the river. The drinking age at the time when George was there, was 18, and there was a lot of partying going on because there was a bar on every corner.

Southwest Texas State University has become a well recognized institution for being a small but large school, if you get the meaning. It's big enough to be respected in business circles and small enough for students to think of it as an extenuation of their high school days, especially in the 1970's when George Strait was going there. But it remains known for putting out some of the best teachers known throughout the world.

George was married with a little girl to raise, so studying and playing dances took up all of his time in San Marcos. Oh, he partied some, but he was focused on getting that degree and becoming a country western singer. With his band Stoney Ridge, he made money on any night he could, most notably Wednesday night at Cheatham Street Warehouse where the beer was 50 cents and girls could come in free. It was very well known back then and politically correct to let girls in for free because where the girls are, so come the boys who have money to pay for girl's drinks. And there were plenty of girls. A whole slew of them took a kind look at George Strait. But he never took his ring off. By all accounts, he was faithful to Norma. Some might say how can a good looking singer not be tempted and sure, George was. But it takes a real man to take it on home. Remember the old saying: "You can look at the menu but you gotta eat at home."

George and his band played all around San Marcos. In nearby New Braunfels, Texas, he played at Gruene Hall, touted as the oldest dance hall in Texas. The hall was built by H. H. Gruene to give his farm hands a place to go nights after a hard day's work. Today, it's a huge tourist town, Gruene, Texas. Shops, the Grist Mill restaurant and the nearby Comal and Guadalupe Rivers are what makes it so. When you go into Gruene Hall, there is a picture of a very young George Strait with his cowboy hat on hanging on the wall along with a bunch of other musical greats who have played there such as Leon Russell and Willie Nelson. The dance scene in the movie "Michael" starring John Travolta was filmed there. Lyle Lovett, Hank Ketchum, the late Townes Van Zandt and Jerry Jeff Walker have called Gruene Hall home. On the photo, George wrote: "To Pat, MJ and Nannette. Thanks for all the unforgettable nights at Gruene. We'll have many more, I'm sure. George Strait."

People who say they saw George Strait and The Ace In The Hole Band play in and around San Marcos say he really knows how to put on a show. But instead of letting the girls hit on him during breaks in the music, he'd sit with his wife or family members. Shy by nature, George had and still has a hand with the adulation he receives. It all started in San Marcos as the bigger he got, the more the girls tried to get at him. In those small dance halls, it was easy to get at the star of the show. There was no band bus to retreat to, no Green Room to relax in. When you came off stage, a girl could scoop you up at the drop of your hat. But George was true blue to his life with Norma. There is no indication he ever took one of those beauties up on a scoop.

Ron Kattner, a fellow 1978 Southwest Texas State University graduate, said that those dances were rowdy and no-holds barred.

"We were kids back then, us against the world, partying every night, but not George. He'd take it on home and leave the drinking and skirt-chasing to guys like me and Mike Bartz."

Mike Bartz was a very good friend of George Strait's. They shared the bars with each other and classes in college, too. Mike was a bartender while George took the stage with the band. Mike tended bar at "Nephews" on the square in San Marcos and at a bar called "The Long Branch." But they did their hanging out at the Cheatham Street Warehouse.

"I never saw George Strait drunk or disrespect women when they came onto him or raise any of the kind of hell we all raised. I had an animal husbandry class with him as well as a farm shop class. After class, we'd mosey on over to Herbert's Taco Hut for some cheap, but good tacos and a cold one and we'd talk about old Doc Abel, our agriculture professor. Doc Abel heard George sing and said that he'd become famous one day."

A wise old Doctor, that professor Doc Abel. Even though Mike Bartz didn't get his degree as George did, he's become a successful building contractor and has been living in San Marcos all his life. Coming from nearby Pflugerville, Bartz married a girl from Washington State named Cindy and sees George from time to time when he's in San Marcos, which isn't very much these days. But they haven't kept in touch as old friends sometimes do. In reality, both don't have the time even though while going to college together, they were tight friends and hung around together all the time, everyday. George did acknowledge Mike with a wink and a nod at one of his concerts in the late 1990's as the huge star he had become.

"If you're looking for any dirt on George Strait, you won't find any of it in San Marcos, Texas." Mike added. "He's a straight as his name implies. When we all stayed out late drinking and dancing, George would pack up his guitar and take it on home. Oh, he'd have a few cold ones, but he was really in love with his wife and little daughter, Jenifer, so he'd just go on home."

"But in the late 70's, I could tell George was getting big and going to get bigger." Bartz said. "When he got a tour bus in 1981 and played in San Antonio, girls would hang their panties and bras on the mirrors and kiss red lipstick kisses on the windshield. Thank God George was already married because he was so shy he probably wouldn't have had the nerve to ask any of those girls out."

Through all the early madness as George was climbing the ladder of country music success, Norma was calm. The love George and Norma shared carried them through those trying times, but George never flinched. He knew his place and his place was at home with his wife and child. There is little doubt that the divorce he experienced as a kid of nine had a profound effect on him and as long as Norma Voss Strait would stand beside him, he was more than willing to stand by her.

Even today, it's hard to imagine a love so strong after nearly 40 years. Everyone is getting a divorce and marrying other country music stars. Vince Gill divorced and then married Amy Grant. Garth Brooks divorced Sandy, his high school sweetheart and married country music star Trisha Yearwood. As of the publication of this book, Randy Travis is divorcing his longtime love and manager, Elizabeth while Billy Ray Cyrus has filed papers against his wife of many years, Tish. Divorce is rampant! But not at the Strait home front. George and Norma are still going strong. After all they've been through, and honestly, they've been through hell and back, more than any of those country music stars have been through, the Straits have used those highs and lows to grow even stronger.

After Erv saw George play at his Prairie Rose bar, George started to get more gigs and Erv spread the word about the kid he thought had something special. George changed the name of the band to The Ace In The Hole Band and they would play all around the University and in bars on the square in San Marcos. In time, The Ace In The Hole Band would play Austin backing up the Texas Top Hands and The Texas Playboys. They'd head south to San Antonio to play the dives there and on over to Bandera to play the old Texas Star. Down in Helotes, they'd play at

Floore's Country Store, owned by John T. Floore who had to expand the location as he booked some of the better acts such as Rick Trevino and John Michael Montgomery. When George and his band played there, it was a small roadside beer joint and you might make $25 a piece a night. The Country Store was just outside of San Antonio but still far enough away to be out in the country.

While going to school in Southwest Texas State University, George and his friends would go to Herbert's Taco Hut to eat some good Mexican food. It was their hangout because the food was good and the beer was cold. Ron Kattner, a fellow SWTSU student who knew George back then said sometimes George and his band played the old Cheatham Street Warehouse, and didn't hardly draw a large crowd even on nickel beer night. So the Taco Hut was a good place to eat cheap when the money from the gig was low.

As in Hawaii, George used the time in San Marcos to hone his singing and playing style. The bars and clubs he played were perfect sounding boards. If they liked you, it encouraged you. The Ace In The Hole Band was well liked. Terry Hale and Mike Daily were not only fellow students with George, they were the core of the band. As the band got bigger and better, they started to make more money. Serious money.

"We got to the point where we made fifteen hundred a night." Ron Cabal, the lead guitarist said at the time; "Gruene Hall became one of the better places to play and we'd divide up the money at three hundred a man for the night, which was big money back then."

Ray Benson of Asleep At The Wheel, a true Texas western swing band in the same vein as Bob Wills offered this.

"The first time I heard George Strait was in San Marcos, Texas. He had opened the show for us. I was sitting on our old bus listening to this band playing the old country standards and this guy had this true country voice, I mean he was downright good but I couldn't see him. When I asked one of the guys who is the singer, he said George Strait. Later on, when I heard "Unwound" on the radio, it was the same guy. He had a hit and I could understand why. I'm glad he hit it big because country wasn't getting anymore country until guys like George Strait came along."

Another hot spot to play at during those college days was in Austin, Texas. In 1964, a cowboy named James White opened the Broken Spoke on the edge of town. It became a regular joint to play for The Ace In The Hole Band. Today, it's still going strong and even has a little museum inside where the stars who have played there are featured. George's picture is in there.

While attending college in San Marcos, George worked as a cowboy in nearby Martindale and on his father's ranch in South Texas. He'd also come home to Pearsall, Texas to play at the old haunts such as the Wishing Well Club, a converted bowling alley on the way to Dilley, Texas off highway 81. On Friday and Saturday nights, the Wishing Well would be packed with oil field workers and farmers looking for an air conditioned place to drink and dance with their ladies. It was the classic country western club.

George and his band would play as far south as Kingsville, then onto Corpus Christi and then, Houston. During the summers when not in college, the band did a lot of road gigs, often living out of a suitcase instead of back home in San Marcos. It was at this time, Mike Daily's grandfather, H.W. "Pappy" Daily, who had managed one of George's idols, George Jones had a recording studio in Houston and made records for the local talent on the "D" label. Mike's father, Don Daily brought The Ace In The Hole Band into the studio to cut a couple of songs George had written. Not known as a songwriter, they did it anyway. The studio had done Willie Nelson's 45's and Nelson's "Family Bible" by Claude Gray in 1960.

"I encouraged them to come on in and make a record." Don Daily remembered. "And they thought, well, they could use it to book some dances, using the record for a promo copy. It got some air play, but that was about it."

The studio was an old house on Studemont Street in Houston that had been converted into a recording studio. The Ace In The Hole Band went back into the studio in 1978 and cut more songs. They recorded three songs George had written. "I Just Can't Go On Dying Like This", "That Don't Change The Way I Feel About You" and I Don't Want To Talk It Over Anymore." These are the only three songs George had ever written that he recorded. Today, almost all of his songs are by someone else, including a few songs on the "Twang" album by his son, Bubba.

"I remember when George and the band came into the studio. He would get right up to the microphone and belt it out real sincere like, but off stage, he was real shy, didn't have much to say."

The songs didn't really go anywhere because the "D" label had to compete with the big boys out of Nashville. And there were still some payola going on so small labels didn't really have a chance. So the band came back to San Marcos and continued to play dances and sell the 45's beside the stage to anyone who'd buy them at a dollar a pop.

It was 1973 and some of the band had decided to relocate to Austin, Texas where the outlaw country music scene was thriving. Willie Nelson and Waylon Jennings lead the way and The Ace In The Hole Band thought they'd better get on board. Some of those early Ace members still live there today while George has moved to the Dominion in San Antonio.

By 1976, George had been introduced to songwriter Darryl Staedtler through Cheatham Street Warehouse in San Marcos owner, Kent Finlay. Finlay knew that George Strait had that something special that is in almost all the great singers. He was a big fan of George's and when he introduced George to Staedtler, they hit it off right away. Staedtler had been in Nashville for ten years before he moved to Austin. He had written a number of successful songs there and he was looking for a singer to sing some of his new songs for demo tapes to pitch to records or the stars looking for a good song. Songwriters need good singers to sing their songs for A&R (Artist and Repertoire) people. It's the musical food change and Staedtler needed a George Strait to grab the attention of those who make the decisions.

Darryl Staedtler liked George's voice so much that he packed him up and Kent Finlay tagged along as the three of them went to Nashville. They drove all night long from San Marcos to Nashville and stayed at the Hall Of Fame Motor Inn on the edge of Music Row. If you're gonna make it in any shape or form in country music, you've got to go to Nashville.

Leaving his wife behind in San Marcos, George's journey to the top of the musical world happened when a songwriter needed a voice. Spurred on by a man with a "good ear" for country music in Kent Finlay, George would not look back in his quest to be a star. And, just as Hawaii had given George the time to hone his craft, San Marcos, Texas gave him the connections to enter the country music world.

Five
Nashville To Austin City Limits

Landing in Nashville, George Strait and his friends made the rounds. Most of the business of country music in and around Music Row are converted houses where when you stand in the foyer, it was probably the living room long ago. It's a cool thing, very informal. Music Row also is home to many of the top record companies and recording studios. George went into the studio to do six of Darryl Staedtler's songs with studio musicians such as Johnny Gimble on fiddle, Weldon Myrick on pedal steel and Buddy Spicher on the other fiddle. One of the songs they cut of Darryl's was called "80 Proof Bottle Of Tear Stopper."

The next step was to get the demos into the right hands. And to get George a record deal. Every year, the record companies listen to thousands of songs from aspiring singers and musicians and songwriters, so the competition is brutal. To get the right people to even listen to your demo is a feat "in and of itself". When Darryl and George pitched the songs, they were told the music was "too country." But George didn't get discouraged. He was ready for rejection and told Kent and Darryl that he wasn't gonna change being country. Since his Ace In The Hole Band was known as a country bar band and they were drawing huge crowds where ever they played, he decided early on to stay the course.

"We were the consummate country bar band." Tommy Foote, Ace In The Hole's drummer at the time who is now George's road manager. "George had the voice, he had the looks and he was always focused on country being played country style like all the greats had done it. I saw it as a way to meet girls and to keep from getting a job. George saw it as the future."

In 1979, Nashville had its identity crisis. In the early 1960's it went though the same crisis when Marty Robbins and Jim Reeves brought in female backup singers and strings and lavish arrangements. Danny Davis and the Nashville Brass was in the mix, too. Then singers like Conway Twitty, Buck Owens, Merle Haggard, Charley Pride and George Jones and Tammy Wynette brought country back in line. In 1979, country strayed again with Crystal Gayle, John Denver and Olivia Newton-John. The lines between country and pop blurred again.

After he graduated from college in 1979 with his BA degree, George continued to play the clubs and dance halls, putting the rejection in Nashville behind him to work on the Hart Ranch in Martindale, just outside San Marcos. George was the ranch manager over 1000 head of cattle, a big operation. He believed that if Nashville would shun the greats like Loretta Lynn and Johnny Cash in favor of popped up country music, the timing for him wasn't right. So he put his effort into being a hard working rancher.

"I was just doing the ranching to supplement my income a little bit, you know." George said after he had made it. "Course, if my musical career was to end tomorrow, I'd probably go back to ranching again because I really like riding and roping and stuff like that, but I will never miss building fences."

George knew he had to get back to Nashville if he ever had any hopes of making it in country music. Many musicians may be from any other parts of the world, but if you don't go to Nashville, you're not going to make it at all. It's the water hole in the desert.

You might meet a good singer and you never know if or when he or she will become famous because there are so many in the dance halls of America. That great song by Gladys Knight and the Pips says it all when they sang "Midnight Train To Georgia" where the singer tries to make, but he's leaving it all to go back home after failing to make it. It happens a thousand times a year in Nashville. It could've happened to George Strait but for the support of Norma and the help of Erv Woosley and Kent Finlay who kept on believing that George wasn't too country as the critics were saying.

There's an actor in Austin, Texas who's been pushing and believing for over 20 years. The only part he has ever received was one line in the Tom Hanks movie, Forrest Gump where he tells Gump "Here, look at this!" He then throws Gump a Playboy magazine that shows a picture of the love of Gump's life, Jenny. That actor is still believing in himself just as his family has done all those 20 years. George was in the same boat in 1980 when he went to Nashville and didn't get that first record deal because he was 'too country." In reality, because of his sheer talent, he got a record deal in record time. Most struggle as that Austin actor has struggled for many years before "making it." George was lucky, very lucky. And, he's been very lucky ever since with a career that has defied all the odds in a business known for chewing up stars and spitting them out.

When George didn't hit on that first try and Norma gave him one year to make it, he came back home just like the words of that song by Gladys Knight. But he wasn't done, yet. He still had that young family to support.

"I was twenty-seven years old during those early days and Norma was going to have another baby. We were struggling and I'd been playing for six or seven years and I was beginning to believe those guys up in Nashville, maybe I was too country, maybe I wasn't as good as I thought I was and maybe I ought to try something else. I had a family to feed. So I gave my band notice and signed up for a full-time job with this outfit out of Uvalde, Texas that designed cattle pens. But a week before I was to report to work, I realized I just couldn't give up that easy. That's when Norma told me to give it a year, just one more year."

That year was 1980. Even though Norma was looking forward to the move to Uvalde and a new house with a steady paycheck, she wanted George to be happy.

"He had a look in his eyes, he'd been impossible to get along with since he'd decided to quit playing, and I knew he couldn't be happy if he didn't make one last try to make it." Norma said in an interview. "George was moping around the house so much I couldn't stand it. I figured I didn't want to live in Uvalde with him like that, so we sat down and talked about his hopes in music. I wanted him to give it one more try."

In 1980, Nashville took notice when two movies hit the screens that brought back real country music. "Coal Miner's Daughter" and "Urban Cowboy" both had soundtracks that made Nashville stand up and take notice about its roots in hard core country music. They made money, lots of it. And, Nashville will always follow the money because it is a business first. The powers that be started to sign country acts again and buy country songs to go with them. George Strait was next in line.

Michael Martin Murphy was the "Cosmic Cowboy" while Willie and Waylon and Hank Jr. were the "Outlaws". Out in Bakersfield, California, Buck Owens influenced Dwight Yoakum to play country music. And from Texas, George Strait would enter the fray as the new dyed in the wool country singer. Erv Woolsey had gone back to work at MCA in Nashville as vice president of the country music division. George pleaded with him to get him a producer who would take a look at him, he even offered to pay for a session. He just wanted to get back to Nashville and get something, anything going. He felt he was spinning his wheels in Texas. And he was. So many bands that are good in dance halls have remained there until they died because they didn't push hard enough to get Nashville to take a look at them.

Erv knew George had the talent, the looks and the ability so he asked Nashville producer Blake Mevis to do some demos with George. They got George into the studio and Mevis recorded Darryl Staedtler's "Blame It On Mexico" and "Nobody In His Right Mind Would've Left Her," which was written by a songwriter who would work with George on many of his subsequent hit records, a man by the name of Dean Dillon. But, the A&R man at MCA, Jim Fogelsong and Ron Chancey still said the songs and George's singing of them was still "too country."

George was very discouraged. But, Erv wasn't ready to send George back to Texas just yet. Erv managed to get Ron Chancey to come to San Marcos to hear George and his Ace In The Hole Band live. There, Chancey would see just how good George Strait really was. He got to hear a solid band with a show that packed 'em in. Even with a great show, MCA didn't sign George Strait. Back then, record labels put up enormous amounts of money to sign, record and promote what they hoped would be the next star, kind of like drilling for oil. The dry holes can put you out of business. Today, anyone can make a CD for next to nothing, all it takes for a rapper to make it is promotion and playing live. Same with musicians of any genre, just sell the CD's like crazy because they're so cheap to make. And you can make them yourself today and cut the middle man out entirely. Rappers are doing and becoming millionaires.

Tom Collins, a music publisher heard the demo and liked it. He offered to finance another demo if George would sing some of his company's songs. One of those songs was "Unwound" and the light bulb went off in Erv and Collin's collective heads. That was the song, that was a song meant for a singer like George Strait. MCA decided to finally sign George Strait, but only for "Unwound" as a single. If it was a hit, they pour more money into George and do an album.

And they were on the lookout for songs for George's first album should "Unwound" hit. Jim Lauderdale sold two songs to George Strait. The first one was called "The King Of Broken Hearts." The second song was called "Where The Sidewalk Ends." George liked both of these songs, but it would be up to the powers at MCA to decide which songs would eventually make it on the album. That was the way it was back then, but that would not be the way it would end up once George's career took off. Today, all songs are strictly up to George to hand pick. He has the first and final say on everything as it relates to his massive career, right down to what cities he will play in.

The decision George and Norma made to give him one more year to "make it" turned out to be the right one. MCA was a great label and unlike Decca 20 years before who said those four guys from Liverpool would never make it thus giving Capital the goldmine, George Strait had broke into Nashville steel curtain where the roster included stars such as Loretta Lynn, Conway Twitty, Merle Haggard and Tanya Tucker. Making it is scary. You work hard to get it done, but when it finally happens, one can't help but have butterflies. Nerves are shot. But it was the dream of George Strait. Few make it in reality. It's a hard business to break into. Some do it overnight and fade out. Others take years and then last forever, right up until they die.

"The irony of 'urban cowboy' music was that when a good-looking real-life cattle roper and rancher like George Strait came along in 1981 with a pure Texas swing sound, no one took him seriously." Producer Jimmy Bowen said. "He was almost like an outcast because he wasn't crossover material."

Bowen was a native Texan who had worked with Dean Martin and Frank Sinatra and then switched over to country to work with Mel Tillis and Hank Williams Jr. George needed a solid producer who would have the vision that George had for his songs and his career. Together with MCA producer Blake Mevis and Erv Woolsey who would become his manager, George was ready for that album. But, he wasn't about to abandon his country roots or take off his cowboy hat like they wanted him to do. Yes, they wanted George to actually take off the hat! The next thing that might have wanted was for George to wear a tie! Not gonna happen.

Until you're a major star, the record company and its cronies will mold you the way they want to. They push the songs, they push the studio musicians and they control every aspect of you. When you prove you're a star hit maker and do in fact, make them a lot of money, they'll began to listen to you, to take your input into the process. When you get to be as big a star as George would become, it is George who tells the record company what to do and when to do it. With the stardom comes the power, with the power comes the money. That is part of paying ones dues to make it to a point where you have total control over your life musically.

If the record flopped, George told Norma he'd be back in Texas and go back to either ranching or teaching, like his father had done. But if fellow Texans liked the fiddle sound and honky tonk beat of "Unwound", chances are it would fly all over the country. Erv thought it would and when Ron Chancey heard the finished product, he said "Yeah, that's it." Was America ready for pure country? When the sales of "Unwound" and the backing album went to the top, the question was answered.

The single was released in May of 1981. The song took off slowly because the radio stations thought it was too country. But the public didn't. They liked it and sales would prove it. When the sales began to climb, the radio stations began to play it more and more. Radio stations began to get flooded with requests from fans tired of quasi-country music with all the lavish production behind it. They wanted fiddles and steel guitars and a pure country voice to cover it all. When George Strait hit the scene, that's exactly what they got. Soon, Clint Black, Garth

Brooks and Randy Travis were signed because they, too, were pure country. At least for a while. That was also the time George had gone back to San Marcos and heard the song on the radio while washing his car.

"You don't know if you've made it big when you first hear your song on the radio, but you feel it." George would later tell a reporter. "And it's a great feeling."

When George heard the song on the radio, he wanted to quit his ranching job and play some concerts. On May 16th 1981 when George was twenty-nine years old, "Unwound" hit the Billboard charts, the Bible of the music industry. If you're on Billboard, you're gonna get played and sell records. Then it climbed into the top ten and by August of 1981, it went to number six. After the song stayed on the charts for most of the summer, MCA signed George to a one year contract and he walked off the pasture and quit his ranching job. He was now a major country music singer. Soon, he would become an even bigger star.

George didn't get to be the King Of Country Music without influencing others to follow in his path, complete with hats of their own. Garth Brooks, Clint Black and Dwight Yoakum all tell stories of how they turned to more of a pure country sound when they heard "Unwound". George had gotten Nashville back to country music where it's stayed since the early 1980's. Oh, it strays every now and then when an artist does a song meant for pop, but stars like Strait keep 'em coming back to country. Look what happened to Garth Brooks when he strayed as a singer he called Chris Gaines. His records sales plummeted. He should have danced with the songs that made him rich. You won't find George Strait growing his hair out and playing pop songs under an assumed name.

In 2008, up and coming country music star Kenny Chesney got the opportunity to sing with George live on stage where they did a duet on George's "Amarillo By Morning" and the audience went wild. Two for the price of one!

"George Strait is truly the King of this business." Chesney allowed. "He is one of the reasons I wanted to even be a country music singer."

George has an ego, but it's not very big when it comes to mentoring or allowing others to grab a piece of the limelight. Besides the classic duet with Frank Sinatra, he's done duets with Alan Jackson on "Designated Drinker" and "Murder On Music City Row" and a duet with country singer Patty Loveless. Duets are alright by George. He's a big fan of a great many other country stars and the up and coming stars of tomorrow can always count on a good word from George. He's been there and he's made his mark on the world of country music and music in general. He has nothing to prove to anyone. And that's what makes him a superstar.

Every year Nashville hosts Fan Fair every June in the summer. Thousands come to Music City and spend time celebrating country music. The clubs are packed and musicians are playing everywhere. There are food booths, t-shirt sales,

71

you name it, it happens during that week and it's a great time to promote yourself or the record companies promote their rosters. George and Norma attended Fan Fair in 1981 as the new kid on the block. It's the place to be to let people see the man behind the song on the radio. When the women saw George Strait, they went wild!

With his touring band in place during Fan Fair, George gave them what they wanted as George and the band played Reflections Ballroom in the Radisson Hotel. The fans heard just how good this Texas singer was and how handsome he was. They also found out he was the real deal, a real cowboy. Debra Winger asked John Travolta in "Urban Cowboy" if he was a real cowboy and Travolta replies: "Depends on what you think a real cowboy is." George Strait answers that question every time he picks up his guitar or hops on the back of his horse.

During this time, George was working on his first album. While in the studio, George used studio musicians in place of his road band, The Ace In The Hole Band. Very true stars use their road bands in the studio. Today, the Ace In The Hole Band musicians are paid like employees and don't do much in the way of socializing with George. Not because he doesn't want to, but it's more of a business relationship today than in those early days when they all hung out together night after night.

During Fan Fair that year, The Ace In The Hole Band played live on Radio Luxembourg that was heard by millions of country music fans in Europe, African and Russia. Yes, Africa has some country music fans as does Japan country music is really big.

It was during this time in 1981 the most wonderful thing happened to George Strait on May 14th. Norma gave birth to his son, George Harvey Strait Jr. They would call him "Bubba" and he would grow up to be a handsome young man today. He would also fill a void that would happen to George and Norma later on that would shake their world to the very core. Bubba would grow to be just like his daddy, ridin' and ropin' and playing the guitar, although Bubba prefers to write songs instead of getting out front to sing them. Later on, the song "Love Without End" was written and sung with Bubba Strait in mind. And Bubba and his father rodeo together as team ropers, George the header and Bubba the healer. Bubba is a true cowboy just like his father and grandfather.

While working on that first album, Blake Mevis and George decided to use those earlier cuts written by Darryl Staedtler such as "Blame It On Mexico." That first album was called "Strait Country" and boy was it! If you listen to that first album of 1981 and then listen to the most recent album "Twang," you'll see a difference for sure. But what you won't see is that both stray from being solid country albums.

As that first album sailed across the charts, "Down And Out" written by Dean Dillon and Frank Dycus reached the top twenty and then Blake Mevis' own song "If You're Thinking You Want A Stranger (There's One Coming Home) hit the top three in Billboard and number one in

Cashbox in January of 1982. Another of the album's songs, "Every Time You Throw Dirt On Her (You Lose A Little Ground) written by Michael Garvin and Tom Shapiro hit the charts, too. Both of those songs tell the tale of respect for a woman.

After Fan Fair, George and his band went to New York City. New York City! Country music in New York City? Yep, they like it too and there is a bar/cafe called The Lone Star Cafe in the heart of Greenwich Village near Washington Square Park where George and the band played for his new fans from the north. They played only four songs from "Strait Country" and the rest of the set New Yorkers were entertained by a real country western bar band as George and the band played some old standards. "My Home In San Antone" and "Milkcow Blues" brought the house down. It's not every day a band plays the old classics live to the die-hard country music fan. New Yorkers got to see what Texans had been seeing for many years, George Strait up close and personal. The next time George and the Band would play New York City, it would be at Madison Square Garden.

From New York City in 1982, George and the band headed back to Texas to play on Austin City Limits, the premier music show produced on the campus of the University of Texas at Austin, Since that time, George had played on it over the years and it's become a must for any performer playing any date in Texas. The show is sent over the Public Broadcasting Network and has become a classic with every artist from Roy

Orbison to Nanci Griffith playing on the stage with the Austin backdrop behind them. George and The Ace In The Hole Band has entertained there many times when they are touring Texas because Austin City Limits has millions of fans watching. It's like playing for millions of people all at once because unlike other shows such as Jay Leno or David Letterman where you only get to play a couple of songs, Austin City Limits allows you a full hour to play a mini-concert for your fans. The time George spent in Nashville and then onto Austin City Limits to allow his new fans to see him live is what made George Strait famous today. When you get to see the voice on the radio live and in person as the fans did in Nashville and the fans did watching Austin City Limits, you got to see the total package...and George Strait showed 'em all the total package.

If you look close to the old videos off of Austin City Limits, you'll see a scar under George's chin from a bad roping ride. Over the years, and with the help of a good plastic surgeon, the scar has obviously been "sanded" off. The videos of today show how, like us all, has aged. But he's aged better than most and because he doesn't have a ego when it comes to his looks, he hasn't had any face lifts like Kenny Rogers who now, quite honestly looks as if he's oriental! You won't find George Strait doing that. He's a little more country than that!

Six
Stardom

When you have three hit singles in one year at the start of a new career, you have arrived, you've become a star, no doubt about it. But can you stay on top? That is the key to real stardom and moving up to super stardom when the mention of your first name is all it takes for the fans to know who's being talked about Cher, Madonna, Michael, Paul, Celine, and Elvis to name a few are instantly recognized by just their first name. In country music and music in general circles, the name George would tell who was being discussed. It used to be George Jones, but today when anyone says George, it's Strait they mean.

In September of 1981, George was back in the studio working on his second album. Strike while the iron is hot or as the old country saying goes, "make hay while the sun is shining." The album would be called "Strait From The Heart." Once again, Blake Mevis was at the controls. By this time, George was being called a sex symbol, a name he is really embarrassed by. Women and girls began to throw their panties, bras and thongs at him when he started to play the big arenas. Oh, they still throw little ditties at him today, but some of 'em are granny panties and under wire versions as George is getting on up there in age. But in those early days of his stardom, the girls went wild over him.

Still under the knife of the record who selected all the songs for the second album, George didn't care. He had made it. In time, he'd get the power to select his own songs but in the early days of his career, he was just happy for the opportunity to make records. He sang the songs as MCA wanted him to. "Fool Hearted Memory" written by Alan Mevis and Byron Hill was the first song showcased off that second album. There was a little movie starring actor Ken Wahl called "The Soldier" that showed George and the band was told to lip sync the song. MCA was doing the right thing, helping to make George Strait become a star by putting where ever they could put him. Col. Tom Parker did the same thing with Elvis early in his career and it worked, although some of it was ridiculous. Any publicity is good publicity. In the movie, George and the band were to keep playing as if nothing happened during a barroom fight scene. That's not far from being true in those old dance hall days like playing the Red Dog Lounge in Freer, Texas where they had put up chicken wire ala Blues Brothers to keep the beer bottles from hitting the musicians.

When you hit it big in country music, you naturally move to Nashville. Not George. He loved Texas too much to move to Tennessee. Don't be fooled, it's a good city with friendly folks. But, it's not Texas and if you're a Texan it's hard to pull up stakes and move away. You have to go to South Texas, the brush country to really get the feel of Texas. That area of Texas shows you why it's such a vast land, beautiful in a way that only a visit can show the real Texas. Dallas is not Texas, really. But you get past San Antonio and you'll see the real deal. George wasn't about to give that up. It's hard to give it up because that part of Texas is so inviting and open.

MCA went looking for songs for their new star. They talked to some of Music City's best songwriters like Sonny Throckmorton best known for "The Last Cheater's Waltz" who gave George "The Cowboy Rides Away." Then Mack Vickery and Wayne Kemp who had written "I'm The Only Hell My Mama Ever Raised" for Johnny Paycheck gave George "The Fireman." The good thing was that MCA pretty much let George pick the songs he wanted with them giving final approval. Today, George finds and picks the songs *he* wants to record and play. But he'll listen to what the brass may have to say with the final decision being his and his alone.

As a side note in 1999, MCA gave George an Australian pure blooded blue healer he named "Bandera." George has always had a dog of some kind in his life just as he's always had his horses. Actually the two go hand in hand as many breeds help round up cattle.

MCA had the money to bring in some of Nashville's greatest studio musicians for George's sessions. When George hooked up with producer Jimmy Bowen at the height of his recording career, they brought in Reggie Young and Larry Byron on guitars, Eddie Bayers on drums, John Hobbs on piano, Randy Scruggs on acoustic guitar, Hank DeVito on petal steel guitar, David Hungate on bass and Curtis Young on harmony vocals. Once again, George called upon his idol, Johnny Gimble to play fiddle.

The one thing that made Jimmy Bowen George's best producer is that whenever a studio musician asked Bowen a question about this or that, Bowen would tell them to go ask George. Bowen knew George was savvy about where he wanted a song to go so he let him make those decisions freely. That's why they work so well together. That's when George realized that the records he was cutting with Jimmy Bowen were in fact his records as he was, after all, co-producer on them.

"You feel the energy kick up on both sides of the glass." Bowen said, "The players loved cutting those tracks just as much as George did."

Harlan Howard, the dean of Nashville's songwriters who passed away in 2009, wrote a couple of songs for George. "I've Seen That Look On Me A Thousand Times" and "Someone Had To Teach Her." Howard is often called the Irving Berlin of country music with songs like "I Fall To Pieces" and "Heartaches By The Number" being just two of thousands he's penned over six decades. Howard was born and raised on a farm in Michigan and worked in a factory in Los Angeles before moving to Nashville in the late fifties. In 1961, he had fifteen songs in the Top 40 country charts, a feat never before equaled by any other songwriter.

But it would be Dean Dillon who would write the great number of hits for George. "Ocean Front Property", "Marina Del Rey", "The Chair",

"Easy Come, Easy Go", "If I Know Me", "Nobody In His Right Mind Would Have Left Her" and "Lead On." Sanger D. "Whitey" Shafer also wrote some number ones for George such as "Does Ft. Worth Ever Cross Your Mind" and "All My Ex's Live In Texas."

George decided to write himself a song, too. It would answer the question should he move to Nashville. It was on his second album "Strait From The Heart" and he called it "I Can't See Texas From Here." In 1983, George, Norma, Jenifer and Bubba would move into a new house in San Marcos. He was going to defy the odds and stay put.

After the second album was finished, George and his band hit the road to help promote it. He didn't know how he was going to be received but he soon found out that he was a star when playing concerts instead of dances.

"Concerts are a whole lot different." George would explain, "At a dance, if the people are dancing, you know you're doing good. But, at a concert, you don't really know."

That's true to a certain extent. But when a concert erupts like they started to do when George Strait hit the stage, he had to have known he was doing good. Today, his concerts are mega events and the screaming and carrying on is much like it was when the Beatles came to America or when Elvis played Las Vegas. If you've never been to a present-day George Strait, you've got to go...it's explosive! He really does captivate his audiences because he's easy to look at for the ladies and he's not a threat to men as it's well known he's been married so long. Never once has George Strait been accused of being with another woman and that means a lot to other men. But it's for sure that if he wanted your woman, chances are he could get her. That's what stardom brings to a person. And that's what makes George Strait such a good man, he's straight down the line. What you see is really what you get.

"Fool Hearted Memory" shot straight up to number one on both Billboard and Cashbox. He and the band were playing the Crystal Chandelier in Brownsville, Texas when he got the news.

"When that happened as quickly as it happened, I felt like I was on cloud nine." George said in an interview with Music City News. "I can't think of anything better to happen to me musically."

The song "Marina Del Rey" by Dean Dillon and Frank Dycus is not as country as some fans would have liked it to be, but it's a good song and when George heard it, he liked it instantly. It became a big hit in spite of being almost a pop kind of song. The next song to hit it big for George off the second album was "Amarillo By Morning" written by Terry Stafford who had a hit with it in 1974. It hit close to home to George as it's about a rodeo rider who is tired of roping and losing all the women in his life to the rodeo circuit. The song hit number four in the spring of 1983. But, the second number one for George was "A Fire I Can't Put Out" written by Darryl Staedtler. That song really showcases George's voice, especially when it hits a crescendo at the end.

George was wild with success and stardom. He wasn't arrogant, just humble and amazed. Giving out autographs when just a few short months ago no one would even care to ask can turn your head around. Now the record company and all the country music lovers all over the world were beginning to see what all those early fans saw in those honky-tonks and bars had known all along that George Strait was a star in every sense of the word.

At the time George was a rising star, he began to play the big arenas by opening the shows for the group Alabama, the biggest country act in the world at that time. The exposure would help put him on the map to headline his own shows and Billboard named New Male LP Artist Of The Year while Record World named him New Male Artist Of The Year. That's what singles do. They get the public interested in hearing more by buying the albums. Because for the first time actual radio airplay was being tracked by computers if you had a number of hits out at once, you were considered a hit maker and the awards are given by the numbers. As with everything in the world today, computers, cell phones and all the other gadgets have turned every type of business around on its heels in the past 25 years. The music business is no exception right on down to the digital sound systems and huge screens that bring the artist right to the core of the audience.

All of those early hits are now classics played all over the world and even in space at the space station! Having two songs in the top ten and one in the top five off the first album and then having two number ones and two other top ten hits off the second album made George Strait a star. In 1983, George and his Ace In the Hole Band found themselves on a couple of tour buses hitting the road to back up those records. They did what most bands do, they watched a lot of movies and played a lot of poker. George would listen to a lot of tapes from aspiring songwriters, always on the lookout for the next hit record.

Expectations were high at MCA for George's third album. But there was trouble on the way. It seems now that George was a star, he didn't like the songs Blake Mevis was bringing to him. And he wanted more of a say in what he was to record. It's an age old problem for stars. They get big and then they get big headed. But that wasn't George's way. He just sat down and tried to work it out with Mevis in a sensible way. But some producers had big egos, too. George's problem with Blake was a ego thing, it was a desire to pick a song HE wanted to record. George was up for a compromise but Blake stood fast, thus the problem continued. It got to the point where they couldn't agree on any song. George believed that he was the one who had to get up and sing the songs and he told Blake that he wasn't comfortable singing pop flavored songs, songs Mevis wanted him to sing. It just wasn't country enough for George.

Believe it or not, another problem George was having with a lot of the brass a MCA including Mevis was they wanted George to lose the hat! No one ever said some of those up high were the sharpest knife in the drawer. Would you ask the Lone Ranger to take off his mask? No. How 'bout asking the Beatles to cut their hair? Never would've happened. The hat was part of the act that was George Strait. George figured if there ever was a time to stand up for himself, this was the time. Even though he liked "Marina Del Rey", he didn't want to have a bucket full of 'em. He wanted country dance hall music, music a real country musician can never get away from.

George and Blake parted ways and Ray Baker came in. Baker had produced Merle Haggard. But their time together would be short lived. But they did cut one album before the split. "Right Or Wrong", the old Bob Wills standard was the title song of the album and was released in October of 1983. George and his road band had been playing it for years and when one of Bob Wills actual players, fiddler Johnny Gimble who lives right outside Austin today said he'd like to play on it as he had done with The Texas Playboys, Bob Wills legendary band, well, George went through the roof with excitement. Gimble would go on to play a lot of dates with George until age and his health caught up with him. And as it had done with Bob Wills long ago, "Right Or Wrong" went to number one, too. The first single on that album, "You Look So Good In Love" written by a trio of songwriters went right up to number one. Even though it sounded pop in its core, "You Look So Good In Love" had the country western instrumentation it took to make it a smooth country song, a great dancing waltz.

Another waltz came from the album and became a top ten hit called "Let's Fall To Pieces Together." To put a few more dollars in old friend Darryl Staedtler's pocket, George re-cut Staedtler's "80 Proof Bottle Of Tear Stopper." George never forgets a friend and one way to help Darryl out was to give him a piece of a hit album. He also cut "Every Time It Rains (Lord Don't It Pour) written by Keith Stegall and Charlie Craig.

Stardom was just a part of those early musical days and George seemed to have it all. He had the hits. He had a beautiful family in the state of Texas where he wanted to live. By 1984 when it was time to do another album, Jenifer was 11 and Bubba was four. All his family back in Pearsall and Big Wells as well as his classmates were very happy for George. Eddie Trevino, a classmate of George's at Pearsall High School said that even today when George comes into town wearing his baseball cap instead of his Stetson, they all just say "hi" as if nothing was up. George is shy about his success and really loves to go back to his home town and the ranch where he is treated much the same as he was when he lived there.

George and Ray Baker had completed ten tracks when word came that George was selected by Academy Of Country Music as it's Male Vocalist Of The Year, an award that would be the beginning of a string of awards from every organization who gives out awards. George Strait was a star now and everyone knew his name, all over the world.

The Austin based ad agency GSD&M had a new litter campaign in the early 80's that was very effective. The ad would use some well known faces to tell Texans not to litter the highways. It was called "Don't Mess With Texas." Willie Nelson, Lyle Lovett and George Strait were some of the biggest stars to stand out on a highway by a red, white and blue trash barrel and tell fellow Texans not to mess with the roadways by throwing out their trash. The ads were a monster hit. And by then, everyone knew who George Strait was. Of course, everyone knew who Willie Nelson was, too. When you're asked to do any PSA ads for the government (Public Service Announcement) you're a star. But as crazy as that may be, George would get even bigger! The next step would be super stardom. When you reach that mountaintop, you are lined up to be crowned King. George had to turn back what country music had become with Ronnie Milsap and Kenny Rogers' stringed and lush arrangements to reach that mountaintop and to this very day, when anyone thinks of country music, they think of George Strait.

The torch had been passed once again. From Kitty Wells to Loretta Lynn to Reba McEntire. From Hank Williams Sr. to George Jones to George Strait. It's the natural progression of things. And, there will be another Reba McEntire and George Strait to come along one day for them to pass the torch of country music stardom to. The old saying still holds true no matter how long you're in the entertainment business. "Enjoy it while it lasts, because it never really does."

Seven
The Good Life

As said, with the fame comes the power and with the power comes the money. George became a millionaire by 1984 and could buy virtually anything he wanted. He bought a boat and he bought more cattle and horses and expanded the ranch in Big Wells to give 'em all enough room to roam And he wanted to sponsor rodeos. By this time, he had sponsors of his own. Big sponsors like Chevy Trucks, Resistol Hats and Wrangler Jeans. When he got the chance to sponsor rodeo events of his own, George brought those and many other companies along with him. Today his rodeos are huge and PRCA (Professional Rodeo Cowboys Association) approved. And he sponsors a team roping event called George Strait Team Roping Classic held in San Antonio, Texas at the Rose Palace. He's been doing that for 28 years now.

Living the good life includes living with the family and enjoying his two children. During the down times, George likes to hunt, ride his favorite horse, "Bear" and fish with his kids. He likes to take in a Cowboys football game in Dallas or go to watch the San Antonio Spurs play basketball. He even took up downhill skiing. But what he really got good at was golf. By 2006, he had a 8.6 handicap. One of the best stories come off a golf course. By the time George was getting well known, he had the opportunity to play a round of golf with one of his idols, Johnny

Bush, not a bad golfer himself. They loaded up Bush's Cadillac and headed to a golf course in San Antonio. Finding it was packed, Bush said, "Hell, let's go up to Willie's course in Pedernales." Willie's golf course is just outside Austin and there they went. When they got there, former University of Texas coaching legend Darrell Royal was already to tee up. So they decided to make a round together but not before Coach tossed his truck keys to George and said. "Go get us some beer, kid." Already a star, George did as he was told. Bush said. "That kid's a star with a lot of number one hit records, Coach." "Oh yeah?" Royal said. "Well, I hope he doesn't get mugged before he gets back with the beer." Johnny Bush said George Strait left his clubs in the back of his car and he still has them in his garage, waiting for George to pick 'em up.

The good life included vacations all over the world. The most intriguing place for George Strait is Africa. He fell in love with the land as many spots reminded him of South Texas. The exotic animals and the hunts are just what the doctor ordered when he'd come off a tour. He even took Norma and the kids back to Hawaii where he'd served in the army and where Jenifer was born. Having money gives you the good life, but without someone special to share it with, there's not much fun to it. George had it all, money and a great family to share it.

By this time George's father had married a wonderful woman named Anna to share his life with. He was happy for his Dad as it can be mighty lonely out on the ranch without someone to talk to. Mr. Strait Sr. had retired from teaching and mainly just ran cattle. And he'd come to George's concerts when he took a notion to do so, especially those at the Alamodome in San Antonio or the Astrodome or the Summit in Houston. And, Buddy was successful in his own right. It seems Buddy teamed up with Jimmy Tymrak of Jourdanton, Texas and started an oil well fishing tool company called Tasco Tools. What the company does is when a rod or pump or anything gets lost down hole, you have to go fishing for it. Jimmy and Buddy's company really took off in Alice, Texas when the oil boom of 1976 was in full swing and when Buddy wanted to go back to ranching, Jimmy bought him out.

"Buddy was a special person." Jimmy offered during the research for this book. "He and I and our wives and kids had some good times together because we made some good money."

Buddy didn't need any of George's money, but if he did, George would've been right there. Buddy had married a girl named Denise and had three kids of his own who loved the rodeo lifestyle as much as George's family did. The good life spread like wildfire through the Strait families. But it was the simple life they liked the most, family and friends and time spent together. In that respect he wasn't your typical country music star. No wild sex parties, drinking all night, roaming around the streets living out the words of a sad country song. Oh that's not to say George didn't drink. Nothing like a cold beer after rounding up horses. But, it's never been documented that George was drunk or took drugs or chased the girls. Stars like Gary Stewart and Johnny Paycheck and Hank Williams Sr. lived out their songs. But, George just takes the good life easy. Now that he's approaching sixty, he's in second gear most of the time. But he throws it in first when he's riding or performing on stage.

Like all good things, sometimes they come to an end. For George and Norma and little Bubba, part of an end would come in 1986. You know, God gives us the world and then sometimes in his wisdom he takes part of it back...but there's a reason. And it's believed that when it's your time to go and you are reunited with your loved ones, that reason is revealed to you and all the pain you went through was for nothing because God has given it back to you...this time forever!

Eight
Jenifer

Most men want to have a daughter they can dote on, mainly to go with a son or two. George was fortunate to have both in his lifetime. While in Hawaii in the army, his daughter Jenifer Lyn Strait was born. She was HIS daughter and he loved her very much as any father would. He and Norma and Jenifer were a team together for a long time before little Bubba would come along some nine years later. So they had a lot of quality time together as a young family. But it's never enough time, is it? Kids grow up so quickly. For the first four or five years, you are their life. They look at you for everything, you are their world, for food, clothes, love and affection. Then when they hit ten, you're not needed as much anymore as they have friends and hobbies to replace you.

When they are teenagers, you want to kill them because they think they know everything and you're an idiot. But after they leave the house and they're in their twenties and see just how tough it can be out there, suddenly you're back in the saddle. Can I borrow a few bucks here and there becomes their new battle cry. But you love them the best you can.

Jenifer was like any other teenager in San Marcos as a freshman in High School. She liked to hang with her friends and took her daddy being a huge country music star in stride. She did all the normal things young girls do. She played sports and had a bunch of friends who go to the local Sonic for a burger and fries and cokes.

"Daddy, can I go to Sonic?" Jenifer begged her father as George's long time friend Kent Finlay remembered.

"Yes, but be careful." George said.

George has always been reluctant to do press interviews which only added to his mystique. Some say his daughter's death in 1986 triggered it even more to shun the media. The national press at the time was unmerciful as they almost always are when tragedy strikes a star.

There was a prosecutor in Hays County in 1986 who wanted to indict the boy who was driving the red Ford Mustang. He, like a lot of low life professionals who see an opportunity to make a name for themselves when a huge star like George Strait is involved, did in fact get an indictment against the young boy of 18. Such a tragedy in and of itself because there is probably not a day even today that goes by that boy who is now a man doesn't think about Jenifer Strait and what happened that night.

The boy, whose name we won't mention here as he's been through enough, was heading down Hunter Road where it "tees" into an intersection. He was driving a little too fast and when he couldn't make the turn, he rolled the Mustang into the ditch. It had been the site of a number of wrecks. Jenifer was partially thrown from the car. She was pronounced dead at the scene. The driver was unhurt and the paramedics treated the other two teens who were then sent home. Even today, that intersection is still dangerous and the county has done little to warn drivers that it's coming up. Maybe the prosecutor needed a raise instead of putting up a warning light?

To know the mind-set of a jerk like that prosecutor, you have to know the county. Hays, like Williamson Counties both butt up against Travis County which is Austin, Texas, Williamson to the north and Hays to the south. Austin is more liberal, while Hays and Williamson "prides" themselves in being conservative and tough on crime. What Hays and Williamson don't realize that there still is a constitution and they routinely, even today, circumvent the 4th, 5th and 8th amendment for political gain. They call everything a crime even when it's not. In trying to call Jenifer's death a crime, George called the boy when the district attorney tried to place blame and told him the boy that he, George realized it was just an unfortunate accident and didn't want the boy indicted for negligence.

"They were just kids going to the Sonic for a Coke." George added.

Few fathers would be so understanding, especially those as devoted to their children as George was to Jenifer and to Bubba. In a way, it's a fitting barometer of the man he is. He won't place blame where it doesn't belong. That's the cowboy way for sure.

Kent Finlay remembers the events of that week when Jenifer was killed. He said the local newspaper, the San Marcos Record, had accounts of the wreck and said they were, in fact, coming from a party, but that no alcohol was involved. The 18 year old boy driving was eventually charged with criminally negligent homicide, but later that indictment was quashed after defense attorneys accused the prosecutor of misconduct. Unfortunately, that's the way they do things in Hays and Williamson Counties. They often break the law in order to enforce it in those two counties and make it where the accused has to prove his innocence, not the other way around as it is written in the constitution.

George's input helped get that indictment thrown out. He didn't want to see an accident become a crime where an already torn up young man would go to prison.

Recently, former First Lady Laura Bush in her memoir told of her automobile accident at 17 where a very good friend of hers was killed. Just because she was at fault didn't mean she was criminally negligent. Again, it was just an accident, a mistake just as Jenifer's accident was.

But some of those friends were older and not so well grounded as Jenifer was. We all hang with the wrong crowds from time to time as we grow up. And some of that wrong crowd makes stupid mistakes because that's what kids do, they make mistakes. Sometimes those mistakes are serious and have dire consequences. The prosecutor at the time didn't know a mistake from a crime and he almost ruined two lives at the time.

Jenifer did as she was told and she had always listened to her mom and dad. But that summer night on June 25th 1986 Jenifer was taken from the Strait family. Back in those days, kids just wouldn't wear seat belts. It infringed on their free spirit. There was no law mandating the wearing of seat belts. Jenifer wasn't wearing a seatbelt as none of the others were either. Why Jenifer died and the others lived only God knows. As in the movie "Tender Mercies" actor Robert Duvall's daughter is killed in an automobile accident and he's left to wonder why all the accidents he'd been in and didn't die left him unable to trust happiness. In time, George Strait was able to trust happiness again. But it took a long, long time.

A strong belief in God is what saved George and Norma from going insane. Although they didn't attend church regularly, they were both brought up to believe that there is a higher power at work in this world. Honestly, it's the only thing that can get you through something like the death of a child, especially your own child. Jenifer's death shocked the music world and punched a hole in the good life the Strait family had enjoyed for a long time.

"Jenifer had so many special friends." George offered, "Norma and I couldn't keep up with them a lot of the time. But, we never met one of them we didn't like. They were special to her, they were special to us. Her very special love of all though was her little brother, Bubba. To watch them together and the way she watched over him made us know she was always safe with her no matter what." He added. "He loved her back in the same way and always will, just as we always will. She was like a second mother to him in a way. They had their arguments like brothers and sisters do, but in the end, she always made Bubba feel like he came out on top."

Her cousins Shane, Wade, Kara, Trey and Walker were also special to Jenifer. There was a closeness between them all that George and Norma cherished. They all loved each other very much and were a tight family unit.

"We will miss Jenifer very much and we will never forget her and her smile and laugh." Norma said.

It will never be known what effect that Jenifer Strait might have had on others during her lifetime, but long time fans of George Strait knew the effect her loss had on her family. It was a difficult time for the entire Strait family.

Just after Jenifer's death, George, Norma and Bubba offered this note to everyone in their magazine, "Strait Talk":

"Dear Friends and Fans:

We can't begin to tell you how much your support during the past has meant to us. Most of all though, the letters, flowers and donations in memory of our darling Jenifer has meant more than you could know. She meant the world to us and we'll miss her dearly. We're doing our best to make it through this and with your help we will. Jenifer was just thirteen and really enjoyed life. She had a lot of friends and was a happy and beautiful girl. It's hard to think of the years ahead without her to see. But her memory will always be with us. We would like to personally dedicate this copy of "Strait Talk" to her memory and we hope you will see a part of her personally in these pictures and remember her always as we will."

Signed:
Sincerely,
George, Norma & Bubba

If George Strait was a shy and quiet type before his daughter's death, he completely sucked it in when she died. He didn't give interviews or feel like playing music or even riding his beloved horse. He retreated from life and no one could blame him. If it weren't his love for his wife who was just as devastated by Jenifer's death, and the hugs and kisses he got from Bubba, the world might have not had any more music from George Strait.

It was decided that they would bury Jenifer in their hometown of Pearsall so all the nearby family would be able to visit the grave when they felt the need. And she was laid to rest under a big old oak tree in the Pearsall Cemetery. The picture of Jenifer on the tombstone is of her in her basketball uniform. Maybe one day George and Norma will join her there. Their plans for that day are just that, their plans. There is, however a larger stone nearby with nothing written on it, but the name STRAIT.

Mr. John Strait Sr. offered this when interviewed for this book at Buddy's grave in Big Wells, Texas.

"You either will yourself to get over it or you get down in the box with him."

George didn't go that far, but he went way down. One of the loves of his life was gone and the knowledge that he'd one day see her again was all he could cling to. It's double sad when you lose a child because you have a lot of "what ifs" out there. What if I'd done this. What if she had lived? How many children would she have had? Who would she have married? Would she become a singer herself or maybe a barrel racer on the back of a horse? What if, what if. It eats at you because there was so much life left to live for Jenifer Strait. But now she was gone.

What can you say about a life cut short? A chapter in a book doesn't begin to tell the story of Jenifer's life and death. But in time, George and Norma and Bubba would move on. George did start The Jenifer Strait Foundation, and he would finally come to some sort of term to her death many years later when he had a number one hit record with a song called "I Saw God Today", where the lyrics state he was looking at his little baby girl in tiny pink socks in the hospital nursery. Time IS the best weapon to a tragedy of this magnitude. In reality, it's almost all a person has as we are just human beings.

George's fans wanted to help George and his family out in some way so it wasn't long before the Jenifer Strait Memorial Foundation was created by the Straits as a living memorial for Jenifer Lyn. The foundation survives through private donations, which come mostly by word of mouth from friends and fans. Unlike other charities, there are no high profile concerts or celebrity events that surround the fund. That's just not George's style. Established strictly as a charitable donation to preserve the memory of Jenifer Strait, contributions to the trust are placed in an investment fund. Each year the earnings from that fund are donated to child-related charities, mostly in the San Antonio area where George and Norma live. The foundation continues to support other charities. A few of those include Boysville, Greater San Marcos Youth Council, Dare To Love Rainbow Room, Boys and Girls Club of San Antonio, Youth Alternatives, Carver Academy and St. Judes Ranch.

The foundation is obviously close to George's heart but he is still so pained by the tragedy of Jenifer's death that's it's difficult for him to discuss it. It wasn't until a few years ago that he first talked about the heartbreak of it all, revealing to Country Weekly magazine, "I got real private after I lost my daughter...I really shut things down."

Although George might suggest an idea, the trust's directors select the charities. Frank Bohman, an officer and director of the foundation told Country Weekly, "Because of the courage and inspiration of George and Norma Strait, this trust has benefited countless young people in need at the same time keeping Jenifer's memory alive."

The first single from George's album "Somewhere Down In Texas" in June of 2005 had special meaning for him. He stated in an interview that he had the faith that he would meet Jenifer again one day.

George's heartfelt and wonderful interpretation of "You'll Be There" is why the song is so special. Watching him do this song in concert always brings tears to those who know the meaning behind it. One of Jenifer's favorite songs by her father was written by Aaron Barker called "Baby Blue."

To try to get over it, George went right back to work after a short three weeks of grieving. He began touring again. He was searching for sanity and anything to take his mind off of his daughter's death. Working is sometimes the best medicine.

But George Strait and Norma Strait and all of the Strait family will see Jenifer Strait again. You can take that to the bank and cash it. Some sunny day, it will happen.

So, after you read this chapter, take a moment to go out there and hug your children if they're around. If not, when you see them again, take advantage of the moments you DO have with them. That is the one thing God has guaranteed us on this Earth.

You know his own son was taken, too. That happened to save the world. And what a glorious reason that it did.

In Her Memory...

**A portion of the proceeds from the
sale of this book have been donated to
The Jenifer Strait Foundation**

Nine
The Change

Some say that the sparkle went out of George Strait's eyes when Jenifer was killed. And, it's probably true. Since he didn't want to do much of anything but grieve for her, there was a spiritual change in him that is reflected in his life today and the music he chooses to sing. His core belief in God would sustain him through it all. He was raised to believe in God by a man, his father, who did. When something that tragic happens you immediately turn to God for help. Your perfect world of fame and fortune is set aside for a reason to it all. In George Strait it is said he decided to live for what he had, not for what he had lost. Friends and families and those in the record industry noticed the change as George got closer to God and to his family. They circled the wagons, so to speak. To help them get over it and move on.

Some of the later songs reflect this change, songs like "I Saw God Today." There's little doubt George would have made it through without his family and friends.

"A lot of people would have gone off in a lot of different ways after something like that happened." Erv Woolsey said of his business partner and friend. "But he didn't. George had his family and friends around him and he had a belief in the Man Upstairs. It was enough to get him through."

George took off in August of 1986 a changed man but still wanting to play and sing to help forget. He went to Great Britain to play the Peterborough Festival Of Country Music. He became very popular in England. He finished dates that had been booked in 1986 and even had a Christmas album come out called "Merry Christmas Strait To You."

After several months of silence, George began to speak to the press again. He told them anything about Jenifer was off limits. In time, he opened up about that subject, too.

"When I lost my daughter...a lot of people wanted to talk and I didn't want to talk except to people I knew and cared about. Nothing worse could happen to a person and it made me kind of back away from doing interviews. I just decided that if my career suffers, well, it will just have to suffer."

He stood fast and hard on changing the way he did business and dealing with the press and he said from now on he was going to do it his way down the line and that if anyone got mad, well go ahead and get mad. The change in him at the time of his life hardened him somewhat, but he remained the good man he had always been. He was never bitter towards anyone anywhere.

The changes in George's career only got better. In 1986, he was named Country Music Association's Top Male Vocalist for the second time at the twentieth annual award show in Nashville. With a lump in his throat and a tear in his eye, he dedicated the award to the memory of his daughter, Jenifer.

Not stopping long enough to breathe, George and his band played a show on New Year's Eve at Dallas' Reunion Arena. It was taped for a video called "George Strait Live." On January 6th, 1987, he played Houston's Livestock Show and Rodeo where he sold over a hundred thousand tickets in 24 hours for two shows.

Later that same month, George's new album "Ocean Front Property" entered the charts at number one, the first time that had ever happened before hand. Erv Woolsey helps pick out the songs, but in George's list of changes, it is he who makes the final picks for the ten songs he'd put on the album. He and Erv go through hundreds and hundreds of songs from publishing houses and tapes sent from other people. They find the songs any where they can get them. That's the reason George Strait has so many hits, he digs and digs until he finds that jewel or that diamond in the rough. They're out there, it's up to the artist or the artist reps to bring out of the hole.

In the changes George made for his life, getting closer to God was at the top of the list. So many stars were dying and the death of his daughter made that an easy choice. After all, when your alone with yourself, God is all you really have, the only Being that you can turn to. Another change was that he was going to live life more to the fullest, enjoy Norma and Bubba more as he worked the shows, did his rodeo riding and the made records. He'd spend more time with his father at the ranch, teaching Bubba to ride and rope. More family time, quality time with the two men in his life that meant everything to him, his father and his son. Oh, and his best friend, his brother, Buddy.

There's something about the true cowboy life in Texas. It's a simple life, hard work, hard play and companionship with loved ones kind of life, especially your wife and kids. When you're raised that way, that's what you know. That's what you do and that's what you want to do. In spite of his mother leaving when he was very young, he had a father that was strong enough to pick up the pieces and teach his right from wrong. He wanted to be that kind of father to Bubba because, like he had done at about the same age, Bubba had lost a sister that he loved. There's no doubt that Bubba remembers his big sister today and with the help of the changes in George's life after her death, it's been good that her death drew George, Norma and Bubba together instead of tearing them apart. It takes a strong man, a strong family unit to get past something like that without taking to the bottle, or drugs or even a divorce. But, the Straits decided that their family was worth more that. Today, so many men and women just give up. Those vows you speak when you marry are true words, "For better or worse" and "till death do us part" are not just idle words, they mean something. God never said it was going to be easy. You will be tested. How you pass those tests in life are what make you or break you. George and Norma together with their son, Bubba, never gave up on each other.

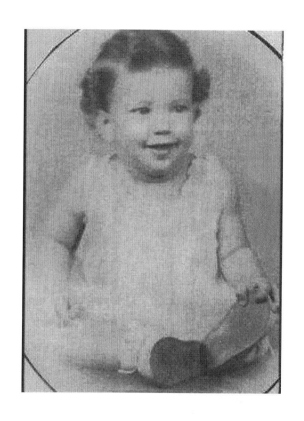

Baby George

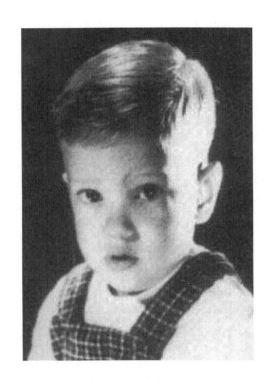

Two Years Old

Eight Years Old

In The Army

Graduation Day, 1979
Southwest Texas State University

111

Bubba, Norma, George & Jenifer

The Strait Family

George and Jenifer

George and Bubba

George with His Dad and Wife

George with His Brother Buddy

Movie Star

George and Norma
39 Years and Counting

George As The "Header"

George On His Ranch

The Wishing Well Club
Pearsall, Texas

*The Cheatham Street Warehouse
San Marcos, Texas*

John Byron "Buddy" Strait's Grave
Big Wells Cemetery, Big Wells, Texas

Jenifer's Grave
Pearsall Cemetery
Pearsall, Texas

*The Pearsall
Agriculture Mascot*

The Crystal City
Agriculture Mascot

The Poteet
Agriculture Mascot

John Strait and Austin Teutsch
Big Wells, Texas

Flyby View of George and Norma
Strait's Beautiful Compound In
"The Dominion"
San Antonio, Texas

Ten
Family First

In the early months of 1987, George poured himself into his work, but the family went with him. They knew that in order to make it, they had to stick together. Norma toured with George almost all the time during 1987 in order to get past Jenifer's death herself. She leaned on George, and he on her. And, the Voss family was so supportive.

In a small town like Pearsall, Texas, everyone knows everyone and everyone's business, too. When the Straits and the Voss families were hurting, it was the whole town that rallied around them. Yes, it sometimes takes a village, but that will never work without the family unit first. It's not up to the village to raise the kids of the town, it's up to the mother and father first. The town folk are there to just look out for 'em. Without getting too political, there is little doubt Pearsall, like any other small town in America takes care of all the kids. But again, anyone will tell you if the mother and father won't get the job done, the kids won't make it, they'll be a burden to the entire town.

Because George and Norma had the financial resources to help them get on with their lives, they were better off than most. That is why George decided to put his family first from now on. Chasing the dream of being a famous country singer was what he wanted. What he got was rude awakening when his daughter died. He vowed to be a more focused father to Bubba. That's not to say George wasn't a good father to his daughter, but those what ifs come back to haunt him that night she went out.

So the entire family took to the road in some form or fashion. Rodeo riding and playing concerts. When George played Texas, the entire Strait family followed him. Buddy and his wife Denise and their three children along with Mr. Strait and his wife Anna. That became George's main objective, to get his family involved in what he was doing. When not playing dates, they were all rodeoing. Since Buddy sold his part of Tasco Tools to Jimmy Tymrak, he had money of his own to rodeo. And Denise and her family in Alice, Texas had Watkins Real Estate, a successful real estate company at 811 East Main Street. So money was never an issue. Buddy never had to live off of George because he was just as hard a worker as George was. Nothing tears apart a family like a fight over money.

Another hard thing about being rich and famous is there is always someone asking for a hand out. George wasn't above helping anyone out and did quite a few times. Take the Round Rock dance he played in 1990 for that injured rodeo rider. He didn't have to do that. He had just made $100,000 dollars the night before at the Frank Ervin Center in Austin, Texas. He did it out of the goodness of his heart. George was very fortunate and his family had money of their own so they weren't standing at the door when he became wealthy. When you work hard and have the work effort instilled into you at a early age as the Strait brothers did by a equally hard working father, it's easy to see why money was never an issue for the Strait family towards one another.

During this time, George and his father decided to expand their cattle operation in Big Wells, Texas. Big Wells is literally a spot in the road off highway 85 between Dilley, Texas and Carrizo Springs, Texas. There is one store, a couple of churches and a few houses. It's a throwback to the way things used to be in rural Texas. As stated, there's not much out there but cattle ranches, huge cattle ranches. Encinal, Texas that isn't even a spot in the road out in the bushes has one of the biggest ranches in the world, some 250,000 acres called the Fitzsimmions Ranch. Most of the ranches in and around Big Wells are 10 to 20 to 50 thousand acres each. George and his father bought more land and today, George has three working ranches in Texas, one just outside Big Wells, one near Encinal and one just outside of San Antonio in San Saba, Texas where actor Tommy Lee Jones has his ranch. Birds of a feather flock together. Success gives you that. With success, you can truly pick your neighbors.

By expanding the cattle operation, George fills his spare time working it with Bubba. Norma brings out the iced tea. Mr. Strait worked the ranch then, but today is getting too old to rope a stray calf for branding. But, the elder Strait still gets up in the morning, puts on his cowboy hat and drives out to the ranch in Big Wells to make sure what he and George have built together over the past 25 years is still running smoothly.

Ever notice when old people stop working, they die faster. Retirement is a death wish of sorts. Mr. Strait has no plans to retire and neither does George. He's said he'll rope and ride as long as his back don't give out and he'll sing as long as he has a voice. If Frank Sinatra did it into his eighties, then George believes he can to. And he can for sure.

As Bubba grew into a fine looking young man, the pride in George's eyes is ever present. Following in his father's footsteps, Bubba Strait is a chip off the old man's block. He wears a cowboy hat almost all the time, and has an agriculture degree from Texas A & M University by the time he was 23. He's got himself a girlfriend and maybe one day, old George will be Grandpa George. It's on the horizon, that's for sure.

The ranch in Big Wells affords the Straits an avenue to get away from the crowds. No one bothers them there, they're just another set of ranchers to the townsfolk. At the only store there, George and his son and father can just go in and buy supplies without the craziest of fans hitting on them. It's just, "Hi ya, Mr. Strait." or "Buy any new cattle this week?" "Will that be all, Mr. Strait?", "That'll be $22. 58 cents, please." When you're a huge star, listening to that kind of talk is a welcomed relief. And, being as shy by nature as George is, it's some of the only times he lets his guard down because he knows these people are sincere. They're hard working, down home folk who may never see the lights of fame. In reality, they're not that impressed with it all because the hard work they do every day keeps them focused. It's nice to have a star drop in, but it's not their life. They try to be as even keeled about it all as they can be and since George goes to Big Wells all the time when he's not touring, everyone is happy with the low-keyed arrangement, especially George.

Country Weekly magazine did a huge story on George for its November 2010 issue. In that article, George is asked what makes him happy, what are the most cherished things in his life today.

"Time with my wife and my son are the most important thing to me." George stated quickly. "And then my team roping event. Roping is like golf, you have a good day and you want to come back for more."

George also likes a good cigar every now and then and a good game of golf. He also likes to sit court side and watch the San Antonio Spurs. But it's the family that makes George the happiness and he has always put them first over his music and his love of the cowboy way of life. So many people believe that to be rather dull, but to George, that's really living. Because he is basically a shy person by nature, he lives a simple life with his family although he has all the toys a man could ever want in life. Fishing with his son, boating with Norma and deer hunting in South Texas are what George calls a vacation. If he gets to do it with his wife and son and his inner family, he finds that to be the best times of his life.

Since the death of his best friend, his brother Buddy, George has taken on the father role with Buddy's four children and Buddy's grandchildren. Denise, Buddy's widow is welcomed anytime at the Strait compound in San Antonio as well as on the ranches he owns all over Texas. That's a true country gentleman. You take care of your family first, then all the other things in life will take care of themselves.

It's obviously hard to be a country music star. There are so many people tugging at you all the time. You are "it" to everyone around you. How George Strait has managed to keep it all together while many of his fellow musicians in the business have not is really not a mystery. He takes it all on home, back to Texas, back to his wife and son and back to a simple life. Sounds dull, doesn't it? Well, that's what makes it work. Don't let the hoopla of being a star get to you. If you do, it can kill you and your career.

Eleven
The Music Machine

There is no doubt George Strait just keeps on pumping out the hits, year after year. Some members of his staff call him the "energizer bunny" because he keeps going and going and going..." The work ethic he learned from his father on the ranch has poured over into his making of music and the albums he puts out. And his shows are nothing short of pure energy, one song often runs into another on stage because he has so many and the fans want to hear them all. George's shows typically last almost three hours as that's how long it takes to get all the hits in as well and the songs he chooses to show off his Ace In The Hole Band. And what a band they are! If you've never heard them, you've got to do it as soon as you can. They are as tight as any studio band. Currently the lineup is Mike Daily on pedal steel guitar, Terry Hale on bass, Gene Elders on fiddle, Benny McArthur on guitar, Rick McCrea on lead guitar, Mike Kennedy on drums, Ronnie Huckaby on piano and David Anthony on backing vocals. Together, they blow the roof off the arenas they play. In all honesty, and surly George himself will say it to, this band makes him as good as he is.

The music machine George has put together continues to roll all over the world. They have literally played everywhere in the world because country music is a favorite all over the world. In

Japan, the bars have country karaoke. In Australia, the ranchers listen to country music much like they do in Texas when roping their cattle. In South America, along with the Spanish flavored accordion music, they listen to country music, too. And, who do they listen to the most: George Strait. Used to be George Jones and Merle Haggard in the sixties, but now it's George Strait and has been for over 25 years. One day, they'll come along another Jones or Haggard or Strait to take their place. But with 57 number one hit records under his belt, it's doubtful anyone will ever match that feat. 57 number one hit records! No one has ever done that, not Elvis or Michael Jackson or the Beatles. But, in all fairness to those great hit makers, they are all gone. Maybe if the Beatles had stayed together after 1970, they'd hold a record that even George Strait couldn't match. After all, they were only together for 9 years and both Michael and Elvis have passed on.

But records were made to be broken. A music machine such as the one George Strait has put together might live long enough to see their record broken, but the upstarts had better get on the band wagon soon. 57 number one hits is a lot of work over a long period of time by an artist like George who knows how to pick 'em. And, longevity in the world of entertainment is fleeting. Its full of one-hit musical wonders, faded movie stars who read the lines and took them seriously and sports stars who blew out their bodies or their minds or both. The one thing about George's machine is that he knows his limitations and how to get to where he wants to be. Doesn't matter if he's touring or ranching, George doesn't get to crazy or in a hurry to get the job done. He's methodical in his work ethic. He plans and executes his business very well. And all this information came from people who know him and work with him. Because George demands privacy from those he trusts, a lot of names couldn't be used. But, rest assured that the words of this book come from those who know. For a musical career that has lasted almost 30 years, a few of them know a lot more than they will tell.

There have been those who are jealous of George's continued success. They've tried to "dig up" dirt on him. The music machine in Nashville is an ugly scene, some of the time. It was going around that an A & R man started some rumors about George Strait to try to bring him down so that his new artist might have a chance to win a country music award. Can you believe that? That it's that cutthroat in Nashville, but it is. The rumor was so ridiculous. He told stories of George doing cocaine and that maybe George was bi-sexual. These stories are so out there, but they had to be put into this book to show how ruthless the music business really is...a snake pit. And, these are the same people George Strait and other stars that lead good lives have had to deal with. With so many of the brass in Nashville still running the show business of country music, it will always be about the money, the bottom line. And, some will do anything and everything to make their "boy" or their "girl" the next country music star. Why? Because it's so hard to break into the business when an older star like George is still making hit records, still being played on the radio and still selling out arenas.

In the mid to late eighties, older country music stars George Jones and Merle Haggard came out front in anger at the radio stations and concert promoters for not playing their songs or booking them for good concert venues. And, they had, to a certain extent, a legitimate argument. But, they hadn't had a hit in a long time and George had hits all the time, every year, every album. What Jones and Haggard failed to do within their own music machines was to find a good song first, then push it hard. They still had the voices. They were still legends throughout the world. But, like a foundation to a solid house, you have to have the song first, then all the bells and whistles such as a performer and a producer. The Beatles would not have made the initial impact on the world without the songs, the talent and George Martin. That combination proved to be lethal to the old timers of fifties rock and roll, not to mention the way they looked when they came on the music scene with their clothes and their hair. You have to change sometimes with the times and Jones and Haggard just haven't found the right song the way George Strait often does.

That's what makes George Strait's musical machine roll on down the country road. The song first from where ever and whoever writes it, doesn't matter to George. A good song is a good song. George has even recorded some of his son, Bubba's songs! Then you get a good producer like Tony Brown who will listen to you and hopefully have the same ideas about how the song should be delivered. Only then do you put your stamp, your take of the song, down for the final recording. And, like an oil well in deep South Texas, you pray for pay dirt! Why? Because you never really know. Some songs seem like sure fire hits in the studio but when they are listened to by the public, they flop.

Bubba was fast becoming a good songwriter. That assessment comes from none other than Dean Dillon who has sold 50 songs to George Strait. He says that the younger Strait has the makings of a great songwriter because he's so much like his father who has an ear for a good song. Bubba has a pen for a good song.

In 1968, the great songwriter Tom T. Hall penned a little ditty that no one would touch. Not only because of its controversial theme at the time, but because no female country star would touch it. So, he and his machine put the song together with a little known singer name Jeanie C. Riley and the song "Harper Valley P.T. A." became a huge hit record and made a star of Ms. Riley in spite of some radio stations that wouldn't play it in fear it would offend some listeners with it message. But again, Ms. Riley and her new machine failed to seek out a follow up hit and she became a one-hit wonder.

George Strait has not fallen into that trap because of his willingness to listen to any song. Of course no one within his music machine has the time to listen to every tape, sheet music or CD that comes their way, but for 57 times, George and those around him have managed time and time again to find that hit song, one that compliments his voice and one he feels has all the makings of a hit record. That is the single reason George Strait is still on top today and is called in Nashville circles The King Of Country Music.

Twelve
"It's Just Business, Boys"

Make no mistake, George Strait is just as loyal to his Ace In The Hole Band and they are to him. But, when you get as big as George Strait has become, the business end of entertaining plays a very important part of the overall success. It is perceived that in their contract with George, even though a few of the band members started out with George before MCA pulled him out front and made him the star instead of the entire band, they are sworn to secrecy. George doesn't tell them what to say or do, but there is a code of ethics within the Strait organization that is unwritten: Keep it truthful and be loyal.

Terry Hale, the Austin based bass player for George Strait for 30 years wouldn't talk for this book. He did offer in an e-mail that stated he "could be fired from his job if he talked" for this book. It's not known what that means or if there is some deep seeded secret out there from all those years of touring, but if there is, the Strait organization has managed to keep it a secret for all those years in a business known for just loving rumors and hoping they come true in an effort to see the mighty fall. Look what happened to Michael Jackson before his death and 85% of white America believed Jackson molested children while only 38% of black Americans believed the story. Even though Jackson was acquitted of all charges, it's hard to put the toothpaste back in the tube.

Contacted for this book, none of the inner circle of the Ace In The Hole Band would talk. Who knows the reason and this book wasn't written to speculate. But it was written to tell a story of a man who may or may not have secrets of his own and has kept the circle around him from straying like a lone calf. We all have secrets in all honesty. Are they important? To some, yes. To others, no. If you're a star, is it important that the world know you like to dress in women's clothes? Does that affect your music or they way you act on the screen? Probably not. Look at Rock Hudson. Up until his death, his inner circle kept his homosexuality a secret. If it had come out, being a female sex symbol as he was, it probably would have ruined him professionally. George Strait is a sex symbol. He may not like it, but by keeping it close to home, it's well known that he thinks the title is just that, a title, no big deal. Since he's a family man right down the line, being a sex symbol is no big deal either. Paul McCartney has been a sex symbol since he was 23 years old. But, after his marriage to Linda Eastman in 1969, he became a family man up until her death from cancer in 1997. And like George Strait, McCartney never let it get to him. Both of these stars have made it clear that their families are off limits when it comes to the press. Say what you want about them, but leave the wives and children alone. Because they are such huge stars, the press have been basically ok with that.

Another point of interest is that when MCA took George in, they left The Ace In The Hole

Band out. George was the star and since MCA was paying the bills, they decided that this good looking, great country singer should be out front, never mind who was in back. Since George was dying to make it in the business, he went along with whatever MCA said. They threw a pot full of money at him and made the Ace In The Hole Band the road band. Just that, the road band. George went along with that because he had to. He never stopped feeling a loyalty to them for all those early years in San Marcos when they were all students in college. MCA's answer to any protest was "It's Just Business, You Understand." The members of the Ace In The Hole Band might not have understood, but with all the great pickers just hanging around Nashville, they didn't have much of a choice. Pickers truly are a dime a dozen in Music City U.S.A. Ask anyone who's waiting those tables for just a small chance to hook up with a star as a road band member.

The one thing that saved the day for George the members of his band is that he didn't find another band to replace the old one. If MCA insisted they find better players to hit the road, George probably would have reluctantly gone along with it because his desire to make it was so great. Anything in those early days in Nashville to appease MCA. But when the brass did hear the Ace In The Hole Band, their collective talent, they agreed that these guys, like George himself were the real deal. They saw that Terry Hale and Mike Daily and Ron Huckaby and the others were some of the best pickers anywhere and that they had played so long with George the comfort was built-in for the upcoming concert push to back the record they were gonna make.

If you get one of the members to the Ace In The Hole Band aside, they might tell a truth that it all started out as a band effort to make it and the mean old record company made the dreadful decision. How Teddy Gentry and Randy Owens managed to come out of the pack after Alabama hit the charts as a signed band is a mystery in reverse. But, they did. Pure talent might have played a part. Lionel Richie out of The Commodores and so many other stars that had come from signed bands in a business that's so unpredictable. Look at Kenny Rogers who was in a 60's band called "The First Edition." Not only was it a near psychedelic band, it turned country when they scored a huge hit with "Ruby, Don't Take Your Love To Town" in 1969. It was a song written by country star Mel Tillis. Then Rogers turns solid country and the rest is musical history. And, where is that first band, The First Edition? Who knows? Where will The Ace In The Hole Band be? Again, who knows? They certainly aren't the stars of the Strait success, although they were a big part of it early on. Now, George can play with anyone he wants to and still be George Strait. It's a good thing George had remained loyal to the Ace band members as he has over 30 years.

There has been a few changes in the Ace In The Hole Band over the years, mostly additional members in George's effort to get a bigger concert sound. Since only a few have ever spoken about the inner workings of the band, it is known that George pays them a salary and that they don't socialize much when off the road. The band gets the play list down and George comes and sings. If you watch George in concert, his guitar is virtually a prop. All those hard days of learning to play it in Hawaii all for nothing but helping to build an early success.

But the business is just that, a business. The band has apparently accepted that. Well, they haven't quit on George in 30 years. But, they do get to do some work on their own when not touring with George. Like Bruce Springteen's E-Street Band, The Ace In The Hole Band does have some identity of its own. When they do play with George, especially in the 1980's and 90's, they were all introduced as "Here they are...George Strait And The Ace In The Hole Band!" Today, the band comes out to "warm up" the audience as the announcer shouts "Please give a rowdy welcome to The Ace In The Hole Band!" Then when George comes out, it's "Ladies and Gentlemen, give a Texas-size welcome to the King Of Country Music, Mr. George Strait!"

The business of playing concert dates has given the Ace In The Hole Band a lot of recognition all on its own. Why? Because they are a very good band, they are very tight from years of playing with each other. Like in any job, when you work with someone for 30 years, you know them, what they're gonna do and how they're likely to do it. Such is the case with the members of George's touring band. They're more than good enough to be George's studio band if he wanted them to. George doesn't need to listen to MCA or anyone else now. But he does. Because studio work is a precise work, a touring band is often too spoiled to let it rip because one's emotion come forward. Studio musicians are a reserved bunch, very practiced and their timing is right on target. Touring bands can go crazy and even miss a beat or two or drop a word here and there, and it is covered up by all the hoopla going on. In rock and roll, there a few bands that are the exception to the rule. The Doobie Brothers and the Eagles with all their lush harmonies and solid arrangements can and do both, a studio band and a touring band, virtually with the same members. Oh, they may add a vocal here or a string there, but those bands have for almost 40 years been their own core of success in and out of the studio.

What's worked for almost 30 years in a successful business situation for George Strait and his Ace In The Hole Band evokes the old saying: If it ain't broke, don't fix it. Both sides seem to feel that way. The Ace In The Hole Band may not be the star of the show with everyone knowing their individual names, but they take home a nice paycheck year after year. As long as they keep doing what they're doing, they'll have a job.

When asked what he does to get ready for a tour with George Strait in an interview with Dale Titus, Terry Hale, George's longtime bassist said, "It's a physical job, so you have to stay in shape.

I usually jog and lift weights. Just being in shape when the tour begins is a great asset."

Hale went on to say, "Musically, I will listen to shows from the previous tour and go over any new stuff off of the recent releases. George will usually call for about three days of full band rehearsals, usually hitting the road at the end of the last one. So, I'll make a personal CD of the song list that George sends us and play along with it for a week prior to those rehearsals. I'm ready to go when the rehearsals start. Mostly now it's just like riding a bicycle. I've been doing this for a long, long time."

As George rose to the top, he was asked to become a movie star in 1992. The movie was called "Pure Country" and did pretty well at the box office, mainly because of George's built-in audience from his albums and stage shows. Played a character named Dusty Wyatt Chandler with Lesley Ann Warren as his manager. The movie was about a country music singer who was tired of the music scene and the rat race, grows a beard and cuts off his pony tail and leaves. But, he'd been in the movies with his Ace In The Hole band as themselves when they appeared in "The Soldier" with Ken Wahl. They were the house band in the fight scene. In 2002, George appeared in "Grand Champion." To show his fans he had a sense of humor in 2003, George did the voice of Cornell in the animated cartoon series on Fox's "King Of The Hill."

But playing music was his love and he was shy in front of the camera, although he eased up a bit when Ms. Warren, a seasoned actress gave him some pointers and to just be himself. The scene where Dusty is singing the song "I Cross My Heart" to Harley where she was crying at the Mirage Hotel in Las Vegas reveals George can be a pretty good actor. After all, the movie was about a country music singer. The only difference in George Strait and Dusty Chandler lie in the fact that George was far from burned out on the making of music like the Chandler character was. The success of "Pure Country" begged for a sequel and in late 2003, "Pure Country 2: The Gift" was being scripted. Would it ever be made? Yes, but not with George as the star. He would do a cameo. And, the movie would not hit the screens until seven years later in October 15th of 2010. It was to be a limited release.

"Pure Country 2: The Gift is the title. In November of 2009, many of Nashville residents had the opportunity to participate in a free concert taping when country singers Katrina Elam and George filmed some concert footage at the Municipal Auditorium for the movie. "The Gift" is the story of a baby named Bobbie, Miss Elam, who is given the gift of a beautiful singing voice by the angels. To keep her gift, she must abide by three simple rules of character and kindness.

When she is old enough, Bobbie moves to Nashville to launch her singing career. Along the way, she begins breaking those rules, even as she meets an honorable young cowboy played by Travis Fimmel. Bobbie found her long lost father played by J.D. Parker and she receives sage advice from her tour headliner, none other than George Strait. Bobbie's ambition threatens to cause her to lose more than just her voice.

Filmed on location all over Nashville including the Municipal Auditorium, Twin Pines Ranch in Lebanon and at Nashville's Northsrat Studios, "Pure Country 2: The Gift" was being marketed to Christian viewers because of its values. Values that are near to George's heart because unlike the fictional Bobbie, George has lived the triumphs and the tragedies of the music world and a strong belief in God was the key to his survival.

"Pure Country 2: The Gift was directed by Christopher Cain and also stars Dean Cain of "Superman" television fame, David Chattam and Jeremy Childs.

George has always supported his "boys." His band means a lot to him even though he's gotten so big personally that he only has time for himself and not much time to socialize with them like they did in the old days when they first started out. As a matter of fact, George and the band will rehearse for a couple of days before a tour, then get the play list down and go their separate ways. The Ace In The Hole Band will open the show with a rousing country song, usually a Bob Wills fiddle ditty or an oldie, but goodie, then George will come on stage.

On the Red Leaf blog, there is a very good interview with Terry Hale, George's longtime bass player. Although Terry didn't want to be interviewed for this book, that interview would have told the story of the band members and how it all began with George while they were all in college together. It would also have told of how things are today. Hale was in fear for his very job in talking about his time with George as an e-mail received for this book revealed. George wants things private so much so that he has obviously told band members to keep it quiet. It's probably in their contracts, too. Any word put out about their life as a band on the road could have dire repercussions to one's future employment. That's not to say that George Strait has threatened his band with being fired should they talk about their time with George. But it does reveal a very private man who will do whatever it takes to keep his life private, only to be revealed when he's on the stage performing.

It seems that Terry Hale is a student of the bass. He teaches bass lessons in Austin, Texas when not on tour with George and is an accomplished jazz bassman. He started when he was 11 years old playing "Louie, Louie" in a band called "Green Saphron Mist" when he was in the sixth grade!

In the summer of 1975, Terry had been playing with some guys for about 18 months when the lead singer fired the entire band. The band stuck together and went looking for a new lead singer. The band was all going to Southwest Texas State University so they placed that ad on the message board at the student union and the library. "Band looking for a singer." On the other side of the board there was an ad placed by George "Singer looking for a band." Terry's roommate was the guitarist at the time and check this guy out. When the guy walked into the room to audition, it was George Strait.

George came to Terry's house that afternoon and a sang one chorus of "Frauline." That did it! The band was sold. Their first gig was October 13th of 1975 at Kent Finlay's Cheatham Street Warehouse in San Marcos, Texas by the railroad tracks where you had to stop playing when a train passed because it was just a few feet from the building. And the rest is musical history.

The Ace In The Hole Band has had the same musicians for over 30 years with the exception of the guitarist who passed away. Most bands don't last 30 weeks. When asked how they stayed together for so long, Hale offered, "Desire, tolerance and a combined effort to learn our instruments. Oh, and a mutual respect in knowing when to step in and when to jump back."

Today, the band has some twelve members, but 4 out of the 5 original members are still picking and playing. When Terry Hale was asked how the band stays fresh for 30 years, he said, "Space. When we aren't working together, we're working with different people in different genres. Also it's very comfortable now to be on stage with George and the others because there's a lot of spontaneity between us, we can pick up on each other's vibes and play off each other's efforts. The things we've learned from working with other players when we're not touring we bring back to the band. And, we all are great at sharing musically.

The original members of the Ace In The Hole Band were George Strait, guitar and vocals, Terry Hale, bass guitar, Ron Cabal, lead guitar, Mike Daily, petal steel guitar, and Ted Stubblefield, drums who was later replaced by Tommy Foote. The Ace In The Hole Band came from the band Stoney Ridge which included Hale, Cabal, Daily Foote and vocalist Jay Dominguez. In July of 1975, Dominguez left the band and Foote moved to Houston, Texas. Stubblefield was also a member of Kent Finlay's band, "High Cotton Express." He managed to play for both groups for a while. When Foote returned to San Marcos, he replaced Stubblefield. Today, Foote is George's road manager.

Every town or city has it's hot spot. Finlay's Cheatham Street was it back in the mid-seventies. The city of San Marcos used to have a yearly event called The Childminders, paying homage to Texas' love for chili. Cheatham Street Warehouse was the spot to go to when that event was on. The club hosted a lot of raw talent such as Alvin Crow, Stevie Ray Vaughan, Ray Benson and Asleep At The Wheel and Jerry Jeff Walker. There was a friendly rivalry between the Ace In The Hole Band and a band called Joe Bob's Bar And Grill Band at the Warehouse. Led by Joe Bob Burns, the band was as good as the Ace In The Hole Band and they still play in and around San Marcos today. Music is a business and competition for Friday and Saturday night dances was keen. Especially at places like

154

Cheatham Street Warehouse because there's only 8 days out of each month to get a booking.

From those early days, George and his band played traditional country music. They had a hard time getting booked in Austin, Texas at the time because "progressive country" was big with Willie's outlaw movement. James White would book them at his Broken Spoke and every once and a while, George and his band would play the big dance halls such as Wayne Dayton's "Silver Dollar Saloon" or the "Lumberyard" just outside Austin.

Mike Daily's father, Don Daily ran "D" records out of Houston, Texas and in 1976, George and the Ace In The Hole Band went into Doggett Studios in Houston Heights and cut the Dallas Frazier tune " The Honky Tonk Downstairs." On the flip side, they cut one of the first songs George ever wrote called "I Just Can't Go On Dying Like This." It got some airplay in Texas and Oklahoma, but not much. And, the record didn't showcase George Strait as George Strait and the Ace In The Hole Band. The label just read The Ace In The Hole Band. That was the way it was back then but, it isn't the way it would become after MCA got a hold of George.

There's a lot of recording history in Houston, Texas, especially in country music and black soul music. Pappy Daily, Don Daily's father and Mike's grandfather recorded some the first material by a kid out of Saratoga, Texas by the name of George Jones. It seems Jones came into the studio and tried to sound like all the country artists of the day.

"George." Pappy instructed. "You came in here and you're singing like Hank Williams and Lefty Frizzell and Roy Acuff. Now, why don't you try to sing like George Jones!"

Those small record labels were not unlike Sun Records out of Memphis. When The Ace In The Hole Band cut their early records for Don Daily, they had the same thoughts in mind as Johnny Cash and Elvis Presley did when they played for Sam Phillips. They needed a record to show that they were serious about playing music for a living. Even though Don Daily was Mike's father who was in George's band, studio time costs money and you had to have something other than kinship to get in the place. Don saw that George Strait had that something just as Erv Woolsey and Kent Finlay had seen it. It was only a matter of time before that "it" would come to the top of the water. Even though George has written some of the bands earlier numbers, songwriting was not George's forte. He was a country music singer. Oh, he'd love to be known as a great songwriter because it's well known that's where the real money is, owning the songs you sing. But, George has done pretty well financially in spite of not owning but a few of his song. And, George is most proud of his latest album, "Twang" where he cut a song called "Arkansas Dave" in 2009, written by a new and up and coming songwriter named George "Bubba" Strait.

Within a year of that first recording, the Band cut Clay Baker's "Lonesome Rodeo Cowboy" and added Bill Mabry on fiddle to the group's lineup. In the same recording session, they cut another of George's songs called "That Don't Change The Way I Feel About You." Some time later they cut Baker's "The Loneliest Singer In Town" and the last of George's songs called "I Don't Want To Talk It Over Anymore." I was at that last session that the band would record what would become George's number one hit record when he got to MCA called "Right Or Wrong." The three George Strait songs from those old sessions were finally released nationally when MCA sent out George's box set entitled "George Strait: Strait Out Of The Box."

In 1977, Cheatham Street Warehouse owner Kent Finlay and songwriter Darryl Staedtler and George left the Ace In The Hole Band behind to go to Nashville to try to make George a star country western singer. That's when they met Erv Woolsey at MCA but that's when George was labeled as being "too country." The Ace In The Hole Band members were not bitter, they knew it was just business. They knew George had the makings of being a star. But, what they didn't know was if George's label would tell George to get a better band. When the brass at MCA heard the Ace In The Hole Band, they were sold on them, too. As George's road band only. When they took George into the studio, studio musicians were used exclusively. And, Hale and the rest of the boys knew that. But Hale is such a great bass player as are the others, they could easily be studio musicians themselves.

As the business of success circled George and his touring band, the need for a fuller and better sound came about. In 1983, piano player Ron Huckaby joined the band and drummer Roger Montgomery replaced Tommy Foote to become the road manager. Then Ron Cabal left the band and was replaced by Benny McArthur and Rick McRae on guitars. Fiddler Gene Elders then joined up in 1985 and in 1987, Mike Kennedy came on board as the newest drummer. In 1990, Ron Cabal wrote a book called "A Honky Tonk Odyssey: My Eight Years With George Strait." Sadly, in 1996, Cabal was killed in a hit and run accident just outside Austin, Texas.

Because the Ace In The Hole Band is so good, they decided to record on their own when not touring with George and does it with George's blessing. The Band recorded a CD in 1994 with Texas country singer Darrell McCall and legendary singer Mel Tillis. They have, however, recorded with George in the studio when they all cut "Ocean Front Property" which is the only country song to ever enter the charts at number one. The Band was also featured in George's movie, "Pure Country."

In 2006, again to make a fuller sound, Jeff Sterns was an add-on acoustic guitar and John Michael Whitby was added on keyboards. Because the arenas George plays are often football stadiums or baseball parks, he added some vocal help by hiring two backup singers named Marty Slayton and Wes Hightower.

When not on tour with George, the business of making a living playing music doesn't end for the members of the Ace In The Hole Band. Gene Elders plays with Lyle Lovett. Mike Daily records other acts and Benny McArthur and Rick McRae play with other touring bands to pay the bills.

The music business is hard and egos often get in the way of what a band is trying to do. The fact that the Ace In The Hole Band has been with George Strait so long reveals that the egos had been checked at the door. When MCA took George out in front of the band, they could have raised a little hell as they all were part of the making of George Strait. MCA paid George a lot of money and George paid the band when toured, but it wasn't as much as it could have been had George shared the MCA money all around. But, that's the way MCA wanted it. That's the harshness of the business. And, the Band took it in stride. They make a nice living, but only George is a multi-millionaire out of those early days. Nothing wrong with that because George is a super talent. That's just the way things work out sometimes.

Thirteen
Pure Rodeo

All of George Strait's life has been either with a guitar in his hand or riding on the back of a horse. He may have become a country western singer, but he was raised to be a cowboy. From his grandfather "Pappy" Strait to his daddy John Strait, George has carried on the family tradition of ranching and running cattle. And, now his son, Bubba carries on that tradition at the age of 28. Oh, boy! Do they have a lot of land and cattle, "I guess when this show business comes to an end, I'll wind up out on one of the ranches and watch the cows eat the grass." George laughed when asked what he was going to do for retirement.

But, that retirement doesn't look like it's gonna come soon. Although he doesn't go to as much rodeo events as he used to, he still sponsors the George Strait Team Roping Event annually. And, the sponsors line up to get on board with him. Chevy trucks, Wrangler Jeans and Tractor Supply all throw their collective hats in the ring. (He often sings about Chevy trucks in his songs) George has been a card carrying member of the PRCA, The Professional Rodeo Cowboy Association of America and so is his son, Bubba. He was able to watch his son compete at the Houston Rodeo in 2006 shortly before taking the stage as the headliner. He and his son are sometimes partners in team roping competitions. George and Buddy started the

"George Strait Team Roping Classic" in the early 90's and it's going strong, although George doesn't grab a rope as often as he used to.

"I can tell you this," Ben Farrell, son of Cleveland Indians baseball manager Kerby Farell in the 1950's and a concert promoter himself. "When you shake George's hands, those are real rope calluses and rope burns there. He's a man's man, alright." But, it wasn't calluses that kept George Strait at the top of the music business for so long, that's for sure.

To practice, George had an arena built all on his own. Being such a benevolent man, he allows others to use it provided they sign a release in case they get hurt. The one thing George has done only once was ride a bull.

"I got on that thing and in two shakes, I was eating dirt." He said to Country Weekly magazine. He's a roping cowboy, rounding up cattle for branding or market. And, he's thrown a few bales of hay out or a couple of salt blocks in the trough. If you've never worked a ranch, all you're missing is hard work. Cattle really don't go out to pasture and tend to themselves. You've got to be there every day and care for them if you want the best price when it's time to make a sale.

By this time, George and Buddy were riding pretty high, their dreams of being able to own a big ranch and raise Longhorn cattle a reality. Since George is a spokesman for Chevy Trucks, he's always behind the wheel of one in Big Wells, Texas or any of the other ranches he owns. When interviewed for this book, George's father was driving a brand new Chevy truck with all the bells and whistles. He wasn't asked if George had given it to him or that if Chevrolet had. Like George has said before, you don't ask a cowboy how much land he has or how much money he makes. The interview with Mr. Strait Sr. would never ask such a question.

In the movie "Giant" starring Rock Hudson and James Dean, that sentiment wasn't just folklore either. You don't ask a Texan personal questions, especially a Texan with a big spread and a bunch of cattle. So, it won't be known in this book how many acres or how many head of cattle George Strait has. It is known that he's got a big operation in all his ranches. On auction day, a lot of money changes hands between the Straits and the buyers bidding for their stock.

On any given day on his ranch in South Texas, George will saddle up his horse with a rope in his hand and fix a gaze on a steer out of the corner of his eye. Bubba will be to his right, saddled up raring to go. That's how the Straits practice heading and healing.

"We try to practice every day we're at the ranch." George stated. "We usually ride three horses apiece and rope a pen of cattle in each pen."

Measured in seconds, the sport of team roping involved two cowboys, two horses and one steer. It tests a rider's speed, agility, and finesse with the rope.

"The first cowboy, the header ropes the steer around the horns while the other cowboy, the heeler ropes the steer around both hind legs."

George explained. "When both cowboys are successful at it with their ropes tight and their horses facing the steer on the ground, the clock is stopped. If the header goes before the steer releases, it's a 10 second penalty. If the heeler only manages to rope one leg, it's a 5 second penalty. If either the header or the heeler misses, no time is given."

The sport actually grew out of the necessity for ranchers to immobilize cattle, which may need everything from medical attention to branding. But, for George and Bubba Strait, it's all about being in that moment where instinct takes over and the world seems to fade away.

"When you're in the middle of a run, it's more of a reacting situation." Bubba chimed in. "You're reacting to what the steer does and just doing what you've spent hours practicing in the pen. You don't think really, you react. You definitely have that adrenaline rush, especially when the scores are tallied and you win."

The fact that George is so good at it and is such a fan, the premiere team roping event carries his name nationally. The 2003 George Strait Team Roping Classic took place March 14th to the 15th at the Rose Palace in San Antonio, Texas and saw ropers from all over the state of Texas to vie for more than $300,000.00 in cash and prizes. The event originated 28 years ago as a small family open invitational in Kingsville, Texas by George and Buddy, who lived in nearby Alice, Texas.

"It was an open rodeo event, meaning anyone could enter, but we limited it to Texas residents only, " George said. "What can I say, I'm from Texas."

"Anyway, it stayed that way for a few years until we decided to open it up to the word. When we did this, it really grew, not only in size but also in reputation." George continued to explain. "Although the years in Kingsville were great, we were looking to make some changes and about 2000, we moved it to the Rose Palace. We also changed the dates to March back then, a much cooler time of the year."

In addition to the chance to take home some great prizes like a brand new Chevy pickup truck, many ropers get to go against the best in the sport. Professionals and amateurs compete head to head. "It's like being able to golf in the Masters tournament." Buddy Strait once offered.

In 2003 when Bubba and George competed together, they ended their two rounds with a time of 15.88 seconds, less than 3 seconds shy of making the top 50.

The bond between father and son is something that goes back to George and his father. He taught both boys to take care of your horse and your cattle and the land you raise them on.

"When you're a roper, you learn to appreciate a good horse." George finished up saying. "You learn about having good cattle and how to take care of them. You learn how to take care of the land and its needs so that it takes care of you. It makes you appreciate more of what God has given us."

One thing that many wondered was why Buddy and George didn't rope together as a team. It seems that Buddy didn't have time to practice like George did as he ran his oil field tool company. When Buddy had the opportunity to sell his share of the company out, he took it so that he could spend more time with his family and on the Strait ranch down in Big Wells. Like George, Buddy was a good cowboy, a good roper and an all around good hand when it came to tending cattle. Selling his part of his business out gave Buddy time to rodeo with George whenever George wasn't on tour or on a vacation somewhere in the world.

As a rodeo rider, George has quite a number of horses. He's got his favorites. One of them he calls "Bear." And he's ridden in trail rides, a Texas tradition where camping out under the stars and eating off a real chuck wagon is part of the excitement to it all. George has ridden in the San Antonio Stock Show and Rodeo and his musical family is always on edge when he does. If he gets hurt, they're out of a job until he heals up. Since he doesn't ride bulls, George has always gotten back on his horse. But, heading and healing can also be dangerous, too. On the back of a 1500 pound animal, anything can happen and often does. That's the excitement of a rodeo. You never know what you're gonna get.

In 2004, George's performance at Houston's Reliant Stadium set a new rodeo attendance record. In such a setting, George will ride out to the stage on his horse ala Roy Rogers to the wild applause and when the show is over, he'll ride around the arena then throw his hat into the crowd! George often has his concerts related to rodeos around the nation. George is one of only a handful of singing stars who is really a rodeo rider, too. Roy Rogers and Gene Autry were singing stars and knew how to ride a horse very well, but they weren't rodeo riders in earnest. Today, of all the country music singers, only George Strait is a real cowboy. Because he was raised a cowboy, it's amazing that he ventured into singing to make his living. In the early days in South Texas, a lot of boys did what George did, ride and sing. The late John Donaho was a very good singer and worked in his daddy's cattle operation in Pleasanton, Texas. And, he had the looks. You can have all that, but it takes more. It takes drive and desire, both which were abundant in George Strait. All of the elements have to fall into place to become a big star like George is. Look at Frank Sinatra from Hoboken, New Jersey. He had it all, looks, talent and some very good breaks. So did Elvis. Without Col. Tom Parker and Sun Record's Sam Phillips, there would be no Elvis. And, without Brian Epstein and George Martin, there would be no Beatles. It takes so much to be an Elvis or a Beatle or a George Strait. All the right things happened to them for all the right reasons.

"After my grandfather "Pappy" passed away, I was put into play as a personified helper with my father down on the Big Wells ranch. That's where I spent my weekends, with him, working." George offered recently. "Daddy works the ranch today at 88, but not as hard as the vaqueros

(Mexican cowboys) do. He bought some more cattle the other day, as a matter of fact."

Since George grew up a working cowboy, he dreamed of owning his own ranch one day.

"I guess growing up in that environment it made me want to have my own ranch one day. I love the life and I love South Texas. It's nice to be able to own a piece of it and continue the tradition."

Although George doesn't spend as much time rodeo riding or working the ranch as he did in the 80's and 90's, he plans to do more in the future. It's always been his plan to settle down on the ranch when his musical career ends. The ranch will always be there for him and when he's ready, he'll gather up his beautiful wife and head off into the sunset.

George spends most of the hunting season in South Texas because of the abundance of white tail deer. He also might take off for Colorado to hunt elk or mule deer in Utah or even to Canada to hunt caribou. He's been on a safari in Tanzania three times, so hunting is a big part of his time off the musical road.

And, he loves to fish fresh water in the lakes and ponds of South Texas or off the Gulf coast for bill fish. He's fished the Bahamas, St. Thomas, Venezuela, Panama, Costa Rica, and Mexico.

"I won't go out anymore when the water's rough, though." He said. "I've had enough of that. But there's nothing like hooking a big marlin."

When asked if he's given up his rodeo riding days as he approaches sixty years, he said, "I don't rodeo as much nowadays. Bubba and I still practice and enjoy riding and we have fun at it, but not professionally anymore. Bubba backed off from it. We're still members of the United States Team Roping events and we'll continue to get to some of those events. In the past we have been able to win as a team a few times. That's what I consider to be my greatest team roping accomplishment, winning with my son."

But George and Bubba have turned their sights to Bubba's song writing career where he's penned some songs for George's most recent album, "Twang."

"He's got all the makings of becoming a great songwriter." George said proudly in a recent interview.

That's also the verdict of Dean Dillon, who has written or co-written over 50 songs for George going all the way back to "Unwound." Dillon collaborated with George and Bubba on two cuts for that album. Bubba himself sounds modest when asked if this is what he might want to do in his life. He'd gotten that degree from Texas A & M University to have something to "fall back on" like his daddy did. It's very doubtful he'll ever use it as the amount of money George Strait has is in the hundreds of millions of dollars, not to mention the land and the cattle operation. But it's nice to have that degree. It's also nice to be able to write songs because everyone knows in the music business that it's where the real money is. Most people don't know that part of the business. If you're the song writer, you make the money off the song, the singer just makes the money off the performance of the song. If you're a George Strait, you probably have a deal that nets you part of the publishing rights.

Bubba's first song on "Twang" was called "Arkansas Dave." (It's named after an Arkansas outlaw named "Arkansas Dave Rudabaugh) Bubba likes cowboys and outlaws and the old west. Wonder where he got that from? George and Bubba like the same stuff, true die-hard country songs and that's what Bubba plans to write. When they're not playing golf together, George and his 29 year old son like to rope and ride and try to write songs together. On George's 2009 album, "Twang", Bubba and his father wrote three songs together. "Living For The Night", "He's Got That Something Special" and "Out Of Sight, Out Of Mind." This collaboration has pleased George greatly.

"It makes a papa proud to have my son contributing to the creation of this record." George told Country Weekly magazine.

Bubba has hopes that other stars will want to cut some of his songs, too. Does Bubba plan to sing his songs like his father has done?

"Not unless I learn to sing. I got my Mom's singing voice! But that's okay, I don't know if I could sing in front of a lot of people anyway."

Back to the rodeo, when Bubba and George did ride and rope, Bubba was the heeler and George the header and they won some competitions together. Both are proudest when they compete together. They have a huge private arena on the ranch in South Texas where they practice roping and riding before entering events. In the 1990's, the Straits did a lot of roping and riding, but today, Bubba and his father do more golfing and watching the Spurs and Cowboys play their sports.

In 2009 for the "Twang" album, George was looking for new material to add to the albums theme of pure country twang. Again, he turned to his old stalwarts from Nashville such as Dean Dillon. Dean's daughter, Jessie Jo Dillon was trying to break into the songwriting business like her father had done three decades before. Dean Dillon has sold songs to George Strait, Kenny Chesney, Toby Keith, and Alabama. George has cut more than 50 of Dean's songs to date.

In November of 2008, Jessie Jo came across an idea for a song which she really liked and felt it was strong enough to take to her father.

"I had this idea of 'the breath you take'." She began, "I heard variations of it in different movies or people saying things similar to it, but I never would hear it phrased that particular way."

Jessie Jo ran it by Dean, who agreed that it was catchy. "I called Casey Beathard who's a good buddy of mine to see if he would like to work on it with us." Dean said in an interview.

"When it's Dean Dillon calling, it doesn't matter what you're doing, you go write with him." Beathard smiled, "I can think of no one better to write with than Dean Dillon."

The next day, Casey, Jessie Jo and Dean met up at Dean's Nashville office to work on what would become "The Breath You Take."

"I was blown away by it." Casey offered. "I have five kids of my own and I'm always chasing them around trying to make the most of each day."

They all agreed that the song had to start with the theme of being a child and it goes all throughout your life. Casey had just written a hit song for Kenny Chesney called "The Boys Of Fall." In a little more than an hour, "The Breath You Take" was complete which left Jessie Jo Dillon breathless at how it all came together and where it might go.

"Dad immediately wanted to send it to George Strait." Jessie Jo said with a grin. "He took the work tape and sent it Fed Ex down to George in San Antonio. "Everything I work on or write is not for George, but it's FOR George, if you know what I mean." Dean said with a sly grin. "I just thought it would be a good song for his new album "Twang" that needed a soft song among the hard-core country songs that were lined up for the album.

Dean thought right. George fell in love with the song just off the simple work tape he received. George recorded the song as the fourth single from that "Twang" album, giving Jessie Jo Dillon her first chart hit. Dean was especially proud of the song because his daughter is now considered a bankable songwriter in her own right and it's all because George Strait believed in her, too. As of the writing of this book in late 2010, "The Breath You Take" is climbing the charts as it sits at number 8 as of November 15th, 2010.

But, that's a part of what makes George Strait a special person in the country music world where ego is a driving force. George has an ego, but it's been fed so many times it doesn't need any more nourishment. He's used to it. And, he loves to see it when an up and coming singer or songwriter gets a piece of the action through hard work and pure talent.

The accolades keep coming for George Strait. In 2008, he was the first to open up the new Cedar Park Events Center in Cedar Park, Texas, just outside of Austin, Texas. He was also the first act in Jerry Jones' new Cowboy Stadium in Irving, Texas. That concert was a blowout with the stadium's retractable roof. It was first opened during George's concert there in 2009. The crowd chanting "Jerry, open the roof!" This was brought on by George himself as he called on Jerry Jones to open it up. Twelve minutes later, the roof was fully open and the stars shown bright high in the Texas sky.

In 2010, George Strait is one of the only performers ever inducted into the Texas Cowboy Hall Of Fame AND the Country Music Hall Of Fame. With all the tragedies in his life, George has enjoyed much more triumphs. He holds all the records, has all the sales, has sold out concerts even after 30 years and still plays arenas instead of small halls in the cities he plays in. His concerts are events in and of themselves. He can pick any act he wants to open his shows. In 2010, he chose the Queen of Country Music, Reba McEntire and fan favorite Lee Ann Womack from Jacksonville, Texas to open his tour shows. That's not putting down Reba, who is a draw all her own. Nor is it to bolster George's draw that some say might be dwindling. Neither star has to make any excuses for themselves. They are long lasting country music legends and will go down as such. These shows are put together because of their impact on the fans who love both stars and want to see them on the same bill. Moreover, the stadiums they play in are all that can hold their audiences. Both George and Reba continue to have hit after hit and are always in the public eye, George in concert and Reba on the stage and on television.

What's not known as it is about George is that Reba is a real cowgirl, a barrel racer from Oklahoma. She, like George, is the real deal. There's a great amount of respect between them for their rodeo abilities. And, their 2010 concert tour reflects that mutual admiration. As Reba has said, they have a friendly feud going for chart topping and have for the past 25 years. But they've always managed to share the stage, the spotlight and the country music charts with each other over their long careers.

Fourteen
Super Stardom

How many stars get to sing a duet with Frank Sinatra? How many stars get their own radio stations that play nothing by their songs all day long? How many stars are instantly recognized by their first names? Well, the answer is George Strait!

Super stardom is that all elusive plateau where you pass by legend and into the realm of the unknown and rub shoulders with the very elite. Elvis was a super star. Frank Sinatra was a super star. In politics, Ronald Reagan and John F. Kennedy were super stars. In movies, James Dean, Tom Hanks, Marlon Brando, Paul Newman, Robert Redford, well there's a lot of super stars in the movies. But, in music there are only a handful that still live up to the moniker today. Elvis does, all of the Beatles, The Rolling Stones, Cher, Madonna, Michael and now George Strait. Ask anyone, black, white, rich, poor, New York, California or even in the African jungle who gets to hear music played and they'll all know who George Strait is. When Academy Award actor/singer/comedian Jamie Foxx sang "You Look So Good In Love" at a concert, he gave credit to George Strait to his audience, his predominantly black audience. That's finding a super star.

Before "Ole Blue Eyes" Frank Sinatra passed away in the late 1980's, he wanted to do a duet with some of the stars he admired. He chose

George Strait and together they sang a duet in different studios to "Fly Me To The Moon." Because of Mr. Sinatra's health at the time, he was only able to do them all via Internet link up. Didn't matter to George, he was a huge fan of the singing great and had been all his life.

"Might sound strange a guy like me singing with Mr. Sinatra, but it was a chance of a lifetime for me." George said after the recording. "Frank Sinatra is a true singer's singer."

But sing they did and it came out great. George had listened to Mr. Sinatra when he was a boy, although not on a regular basis. When you get that kind of chance, when you get picked by a super star, you go with it. Frank Sinatra did the same thing with Elvis Presley on the old Steve Allen Show in the late 1950's where Frank sang one of Elvis' hits at the same time Elvis sang one of Frank's. It was a smash and did nothing but help each other attract a new audience. By singing with Sinatra, a new audience was opened up to George that might not ever buy a country music record or may have never heard of George Strait.

In the early 2000's because of the changes in electronics, Sirius Radio was born. On Sirius, listeners subscribe to their service and get to listen to their favorite singers all day long. Each singer or group has their own radio station. When Sirius came on line, Led Zepplin, The Beatles, Elvis and George Strait were the first four acts available to purchase. Country music fans could subscribe and listen to George all day long, 24 hours a day, 365 days a year. Every song, any song and just George Strait singing.

Cher, Elvis, Mick, Madonna, John, Paul, George and Ringo, Celine, Diana, Stevie, Michael and Frank are all singers who you instantly recognize and never had to ask who's being discussed. George is right up there with them. He's been a Jeopardy question on the game show where all the contestants knew who he was and what he did for a living. He's been given every honor there is. He's gone to the White House to eat with the President. He's met world leaders. And through it all, George Strait has remained humble to a fault. He could be flashy, but that's not his style. When someone called him a super star, he just shucked it off. But that's what he's become to not just country music fans, but to anyone and everyone who loves music in general.

Ask anyone with the exception of a few whose egos are out there anyway, how they feel when they are called a super star and they'll say one word: Embarrassed. It's embarrassing to have people stare at you and fawn over you and go crazy when you are around. That's why super stars like George Strait like to stay close to home.

Take a look at any interview given by Paul McCartney. He is as nervous as the interviewer. And have you ever seen an interview with some super stars where they have the same twitch or mannerism they have in all the interviews they give? McCartney rubs his right cheek with his forefinger. John Lennon used to mug for the camera mockingly. So did Mohammad Ali. George Strait just smiles and shrugs it off, embarrassed by all the attention. But that's what you get when you reach super stardom. You are it. You are the focus in the room. It's all about YOU. Think how hard that would be? Now think how hard it is for George Strait because he's such a private and shy man anyway?

Another reason George and a few super stars don't want the label is safety. Look what happened to John Lennon. It's hard to be a super star and be safe. Sam Walton, the man behind Wal*Mart said that was the number one reason he didn't like being called a super star billionaire merchant. Safety. For himself. For his family. And he hated the annual Forbes Richest Man In The World List of which he headed right up until his death in 1992.

George Strait is like that. Safety for his family is very important to him. Luckily, when he goes back home to Pearsall or to his ranch in Big Wells, he's not bothered. It's kind of an unwritten rule where the town's citizens respect that he would like to be left alone. A friendly "hi" or "hi ya doin'" is good enough for George.

"If George sees you on the street and knows you, he'll stop and say hi to you." Eddie Trevino said. He graduated from high school with George. "He's asked me what kind of music he should be on the look-out for and what kind of music I was listening to nowadays." Trevino added.

When interviewed for this book, Trevino said that he'd have to talk to George before he told any High School war stories but did allow that none of them were out of the ordinary of what most kids were doing back then. That's the kind of hometown loyalty George has been given by those who grew up with him. Because George is a down home person, he's always welcomed in Pearsall, Texas because he doesn't come home with a great deal of fanfare.

Being the kind of man George is, you don't want to tick him off. Shy people tend to keep things inside most of the time, but when they are riled, they can come at you like a coiled up snake. There's not much that riles George Strait up. He just lets it flow on down the river. Although not a vengeful man by any means, he does have feelings like anyone else. After he had made it big, the town of Pearsall erected four large signs on the four incoming roads leading into the city that stated: "Welcome To Pearsall, Texas The Home Of George Strait." He immediately called the Pearsall Chamber of Commerce and asked them to take the signs down. It seems back when George was paying his dues at the old Wishing Well Club, the city had celebrations from time to time and he was never booked to play the dances. He sure could have used the money as those city sponsored dances paid pretty well. They always hired someone from out of town. One year, the city even hired David Riley and The Western Hearts from nearby Jourdanton, Texas who often shared the stage at the Wishing Well Club just out of the city limits. But, George will tell you he asked the city to take the signs down for the safety of his family who still lived there. There's probably a little truth to both stories. He didn't want people stopping by his father's house for a chat. Since Mr. Strait is getting on in years, that can be understood. George doesn't want anyone bothering his father. For this book, Mr. John Strait was most gracious mainly because he was approached by someone who knew his family and those who had worked with them over the years.

Pearsall is a peaceful town, real down home country where life is a bit slower than the big city. They like it that way and having a lot of reporters and the like really doesn't mesh with them and their pace in life. Since the story of George Strait's life is an open book about town and most everyone knows George on a personal basis, they take his fame in stride. Every once in a while a reporter will show up to get background for an article in a national magazine, but the town is low-keyed about it all. No one makes a fuss over their famous alumni.

When you're a super star, you have to be cautious. Today, George and his wife Norma live in the gated community outside of San Antonio known as the Dominion. Famous millionaire heart surgeons, millionaire businessmen and women live there who not only want their privacy, but want to live in a safe environment. You can't even drive up to the gates! It's like a fortress with tight security and guards all around. It's sad that stars have to be that careful today but with deaths such as John Lennon's murder just outside his home in New York City, well, you just can't be too careful in today's world. That's the one reason George lives there, to protect himself and his family.

With all the crazy people out there, who can blame them? When former President George Bush bought a house in Dallas, the city voted to close the street in the cul-de-sac and put up a gate to protect him. When he would go to his ranch in Crawford, Texas, the farm to market road would be sealed off, only letting the farmers and ranchers who lived there access to their homes. Same with George Bush Sr. in Houston, Texas. And since 9-ll, protecting the rich and famous is double duty. George Strait is no exception. Since he's been a super star, he's been needed to be protected.

At a concert in Iowa, a female fan was so taken by George that she ran up on stage, grabbed his hat and wrapped her legs and arms around him so tight it took four security men to get her off of him! George just laughed it off, but that is a very real situation. What if that fan...? Security is always tight at all of his shows. Some fans may not like it, not being able to shake his hand from the stage and take it as a shun, but it's not. It's for safety reason. Who knows when a fan, crazed with excitement, just might pull George Strait off the stage!

No one can blame George for shunning the adulation that being a super star brings. Some stars just love it. They would get mad if their fans *didn't* paw all over them. But it's getting tougher out there to allow fans to get close to you. Super stars like George Strait have to be careful. Since his shows are so big and are in huge arenas, it has become necessary for George to take extra precautions to protect himself and his Ace In The Hole Band.

That is the one thing good about South Texas. It's so vast and wide open, George feels safe being there. There's so few people to bother him and if George knows you while he's there, he'll just act like there's no big deal. That's the way his father is today. In the interview with George's father, Mr. Strait was as open and nice as he could be. So he's got a famous super star son. Big deal. But can he get those steers in the pen for auction the next day before the sun goes down? That's the only question!

Mr. Strait is from the old school where becoming a star is about as attainable as becoming President Of The United States. Hard work is the order of the day and becoming a super star as his son has become is just a fluke to a man like John Strait because that generation grew up believing that you were never going to make a living just playing music. Those were pipe dreams to that generation. But it does happen. In Loretta Lynn's first autobiography, she told of her father's wariness at her going off with her husband Doolittle Lynn to chase the dream of a country music singer. All Mr. Webb (Loretta's father's name) knew was the handle of a coal shovel. Those singers the Webb family would listen to on their old RCA Victor radio were dreamers to a man like Mr. Webb. The same with Mr. Strait. That is why he was so dead-set in seeing George get his degree so if

181

this singing dream of his didn't pan out, he could get a job teaching. Hard-core conservative living. Practical. Down-to-Earth. If you look at the lives George Strait and Loretta Lynn have lived, it's for sure their fathers played no small role in forming them into believing in those same down-to-Earth conservative values.

For his latest tour, George wanted to have a blow out guest list, one that would show case country music. And what better way to do that than have the new Queen of Country Music, Reba McEntire. If the King torch is passed from Hank Williams Sr. to George Jones and now to George Strait, then the Queen torch has passed from Kitty Wells to Loretta Lynn and now to Reba McEntire.

McEntire, a true cowgirl just like George is a cowboy, was a barrel racing winner with a solid vocal ability when she hit Nashville in the 1980's. Pretty with flaming red hair, she has gone on to star in a sitcom entitled "Reba." And she has a string of hit records, much like her predecessors. Her influences were Loretta Lynn and Tammy Wynette. And like George, she's been married a long time to her second husband, Narvel. They have a ranch in her native Oklahoma as well as a place in Nashville.

The 2010 Tour George Strait With Reba McEntire was supported by a great country singer in her own right, Lee Ann Womack. People who saw the show said it was just that, a blowout! Class right down the line. High energy and great country music. Many fans would just get up and start dancing right there in the arena and were welcomed to do it. George and Reba would give a little smile when they saw how much their music made their fans want to get up and dance, just like in the old dance hall days where they both got their starts.

In 2008, George Strait showcased an up and coming band called Little Big Town at a concert in Austin, Texas' Frank Ervin Center. He likes to give those who have talent a chance to be seen and heard because he knows how hard it is to break into the music business. Bands like Lady Antebellum and Little Big Town are so full of talent and ability that all they needed was some exposure. What better exposure than to share the stage with George Strait? That kind of exposure can't be bought. And, when George calls on you to take a tour with him, you have just hit the proverbial jackpot.

George recent tour showcases Reba McEntire and Lee Ann Womack. He's also had tours with Blake Shelton as an opener and shared the stage with Alan Jackson when they talked about "Murder On Music City Row." George is not threatened by other acts that are almost as big as he is. In fact, he embraces them and does what he can to help them along. His ego has been well taken care of over the past 30 years and he has little more to prove musically.

That duet by Alan Jackson and George Strait had special meaning for the old acts of country music like George Jones and Merle Haggard. For years, Jones and Haggard have been lamenting the business end in Nashville for lack of airtime and basic exposure. Both Alan and

George saw this as a very legitimate gripe on the part of Jones and Haggard. They weren't getting played and the powers that be in Nashville were forgetting who brought them to the dance. The song tells the story of how Nashville's treatment of the old guard. And there'll come a day when Alan Jackson and George Strait's records won't be played as much in favor of the next Jones or Haggard or Strait or Jackson. It's the natural circle of the entertainment business where some just have a hard time accepting the change that is certain to come around.

George's concerts are more than a dance now days. They are events. In the huge arenas he plays, the Ace In The Hole Band comes on and starts the show with Bob Wills' "Deep In The Heart Of Texas." Then the announcer calls out: "Please make welcome Mr. George Strait and his Ace In The Hole Band!" And, the place goes nuts unlike a old Beatles concert. The lights, the sounds, the crazed fans all make for an event that one won't soon forget. When the band and George are clicking on all cylinders, it's a true musical experience.

Entering super stardom affords you a lot of perks. And you get to do the things you want to do and to not do the things you don't want to do. In the past years, much to a publicist's nightmare, George has turned down "The Tonight Show" starring Jay Leno, "Late Night With David Letterman" and "Entertainment Tonight." He really doesn't need them to boost his career, but he will talk to country related venues such as Country Weekly magazine where in 2006, they had a piece entitled "George Strait really can talk!" In the same magazine in 2008, he spoke of the people who mean the most to him which always began with his family. He won't talk about Buddy or his death in 2009. Or, of his mother. And, Jenifer's death has always been off limits mainly because what can you say about it? She died and it nearly killed him and his wife, too. That is the kind of pain you'll take with you to your grave. There's really nothing a man can say that the tragedy itself doesn't speak to.

The one legacy that George has left country music is that there is a definite line to it all now, no gray areas. With Toby Keith, Keith Urban and Kenny Chesney all trying to turn back the clock to a more rock oriented country sound with wild guitar licks and explosive drum back beats, George Strait is who you will always go to when you want real country music. Taylor Swift? Not country. Loretta Lynn is country. Even the great "country" band Lady Antebellum is straying from country and flavoring their music with pop. But, not George Strait. Nothing wrong with it all, but the definition has been in place ever since George Strait took the country music baton from George Jones. And it's actually helped up and coming acts trying to break into the business. The record companies now have a definite choice when signing and placing acts. If an act is "too country" in today's market, that's ok because George Strait paved the way for acceptance into that genre. Being too country is not a liability now but an asset.

But, even these country music information venues get a little bit crazy and began to look more like those old Tiger Beat magazines of the 1960's with the Beatles and the Monkees on their covers. Recently, Country Weekly magazine put out a poll as to who was the sexiest man and sexiest woman in country music. (George came in at #8 even though he is approaching 60!) That's a little on the childish side and tends to play into the younger Taylor Swift audience they are hoping to tap in to. Again, it's just business on their part. But it's a part of the business that tends to leave out the older legends like George Jones and Merle Haggard. For some unknown reason, it doesn't leave George Strait out as he has fans old and young.

That same issue of Country Weekly asks the fans for the most beautiful in country music. Now there are a lot of beautiful women singing country music. Faith Hill, Carrie Underwood Alison Krauss and Terri Clark just to name a few. The list even had Dolly Parton and Reba McEntire on it! But the poll is fan-driven and is geared to sell magazines by participation. It's an age old ploy and always seems to work as the fans have their favorites for whatever reasons, looks, talent, songs, you name it. George has always enjoyed being at the top of these polls and he continues to be. But, being the most handsome man in country music doesn't fit with his shy, conservative nature. He'll be the first to tell you that.

On Utube, George's music still gets "hits" for the old songs, too. "Check Yes Or No" has over 3 million hits while "You Look So Good In Love" has a million hits. People still love George's old hits and his box sets of CD's are still huge sellers. Young people buy his records and go to his concerts even today because in spite of what Jones and Haggard have done to their careers where they don't sell many records as they used to, George Strait sells records by the millions every time he puts one out and his old records sell in the millions due to play time on web site such as U Tube where the younger fans search for something new to listen to.

With super stardom comes the toys. And George is no different than any other star when it comes to getting the things he wants. George owns four homes in Texas and one in Nashville. His seaside home in Rockport, Texas is huge, right on the water where his fishing yacht, "Day Money" is docked. The palm trees that line his walkway are huge and sway with the gentle breeze coming off the Gulf Of Mexico across what is known as Key Allegro.

George has a huge private jet to take him to shows or on vacation. And, his main home in San Antonio's "The Dominion" is nothing short of a compound as the picture in this book reveals from an bird's eye view. Professional wrestler "Stone Cold" Steve Austin lives there as does former Spurs Hall Of Fame basketball player David Robinson. The Dominion has 33 acres of man-made lakes and a professional golf course that plays host to the Sr. PGA Tour Event. The gated subdivision is bordered by Leon

Springs and The Mustang Reserve to the south. Sea World and Six Flags Fiesta Texas are nearby.

The Dominion has nearly 3,000 residents. Every home is per-wired for fire, burglary and heath protection. It's one of the safest spots in all of Texas and you won't be able to just "drop by" for a visit with George and Norma.

Being a super star also means fans, lots of them. There are over 10 fan sites on the web just for George Strait. Straitjacket and Becca's Way Too Cool George Strait pages are the best of the lot. And, you have endorsements, lots of endorsement deals. Resistol hats. Wrangler Jeans along with Minnesota Quarterback Brett Farve, Chevy pickups. And Justin boots. There are even a pair of specially made Justin boots called The Cotulla Ropers, named after the small city to the south of Pearsall and a little to the East of George's South Texas ranch. Just as Michael Jordan and Tiger Woods have their huge product endorsement deals, so does George Strait. And, he is very loyal to those products. You won't see George wearing any Lee brand jeans or driving a Ford pickup truck. When he puts his name to a product, you can bet it's not only a good product, but it's one that George actually uses every day.

So how do you hide hundreds of millions of dollars from Uncle Sam? You invest! George Strait owns a number of companies. He has a company called Strait Promotions which handles all t-shirts and ball caps etc. Sales at his shows and beyond. He owns a trucking company called George Strait Transit Company that hauls his equipment around to the shows. He owns George Strait Film Productions, Inc. which shoots all his concerts as well as Southbound Golf and South Texas Pet Products, Inc. He loves to play golf and he's good at it and the welfare of all animals are of a top concern to George.

His roping event is held at his San Antonio Rose Palace, Inc. And his money is protected through a company called Leon Creek Holdings, L.L.C. This company is run like a conservative entity because after what happened to Willie Nelson and the tax man in the 1990's, George doesn't want any part of that. Relying on accountants who are star struck and will tell you what you want to hear, George's Leon Creek Holdings keeps all of his business as straight as his name implies.

In short, George Strait is a conglomerate and his business sense has made him an extremely wealthy man in the range of two to three hundred million dollars over the past 30 years. And 98% of that without owning the songs he sings! Now that is a feat in and of itself. It's for sure that George has told Bubba to pursue writing if he doesn't want to sing the songs he writes because, as stated before, owning the songs is where the money is at. The Irving Berlin estate is still making money off of "White Christmas" while the Bing Crosby estate, the man who sang the song, is not.

Some music stars who don't own their own music go bankrupt when their careers come to an end. You hear it all the time. They may make millions during their lifetimes on the stage, but if they haven't invested well or if some shyster accountant has short-changed them, they could end up playing those old small dance hall again just to put food on the table. Don't see that happening to George Strait because he's invested very well. His cattle and ranching holdings alone would keep him a very rich man should that bottom fall out of his musical career. Don't see that happening either!

One of those who penned a few songs in his career is Johnny Rodriquez. But today, Johnny is playing those same old street dances because of his drug habit and drinking days. He didn't invest well and ran through a boat load of money in the past 40 years. Chuck Neron of Three Dog Night, the pop-rock band of the seventies who had so many hit records, went through $40 million dollars! Since he didn't own the songs he sung, he is now playing small clubs. Thank God he's finally clean and sober but his career has suffered greatly because of his bad investments and drug abuse. Because George Strait has invested well and is still a top draw today at the age of 58, he'll no doubt have very little to worry about.

Fifteen
Death Times Two

On April 10th, 2009, tragedy would come to George's life once again. His best friend, his rodeo riding partner all his life, his only brother John Byron "Buddy" Strait Jr. was found dead at the La Quinta Motor Inn on Ralph Fair Road near interstate 10, just down the road from George's home at the Dominion in San Antonio, Texas. In town on business, Buddy was tired and decided to stay overnight instead of heading back to Alice, Texas where he lived. A hotel maid found his body the next day. His body was taken down to the morgue where an autopsy was performed to determined the cause of death.

The news of Buddy's death spread like wildfire throughout the country music community. Most were from sympathetic fans, but some of the more probing reports jumped the gun by saying it was a drug overdose on Buddy's part. They're thinking was this Strait cannot be that straight, there has to be a flaw in this all-American family and George's brother Buddy is it!

When the report was completed, it was sealed from the public. That only added fuel to their fire. In their shock, the Strait family asked that their privacy be respected. That's why the autopsy was sealed in the first place, not because of some sinister plan to cover up anything. Later on, under the freedom of information act, the report was opened and revealed that Buddy had died of a methadone-induced heart attack. When the reporters heard that, they went wild again as methadone is a drug that is widely used by dope heads to get high. Again, that wasn't the case in the death of Buddy Strait.

Methadone is a synthetic opiate or man-made narcotic that is used mainly as a pain killer but is also used to treat heroin addicts coming down from a high. It is hard on the heart. But there is no indication whatsoever that Buddy Strait was trying to kick a heroin habit. In fact, Buddy was taking the drug in all probability to ease the pain of an old rodeo injury. There has never been anyone to say that any of the Straits ever took drugs of any kind, not even pot. A doctor in San Antonio tried to explain the taking of methadone to the general public. So many drugs are used for so many different reasons.

"Methadone can cause a QT prolongation." Dr. John Dennison of the San Antonio Treatment Center said. "This is an electrical conduction abnormally which can essentially cause the heart to stop pumping blood into the bloodstream and in essence creates a heart attack."

Buddy's death was officially ruled an accident. It wasn't a suicide nor was it a drug overdose as reported by some of the media. He was taking a prescribed drug for pain and obviously his heart couldn't take it. His age had something to do with it, too. A lot of people take prescribed drugs but often don't watch how their bodies are reacting to the drugs themselves. Michael Jackson, Elvis Presley and so many others believe that just because a doctor said it was all right to take them, they either take too much or they fail to see what the drugs are doing to them as they are taking them. Buddy was getting on up there in years and in trying to ease his physical pain, his body just couldn't handle it.

When Buddy died, George was of course, devastated. He asked the public for privacy and they responded. The media, upon learning that Buddy's death was in fact an accident, backed off. They knew how George Strait valued his privacy and the media of San Antonio, Texas was more than gracious towards his plea. That turned out to be the key in George and other family member's effort to get past Buddy's death and carry on. George knew that the media, if not asked for some space, just might try to turn his brother's death to sell newspapers as they had done so many times with other celebrities or celebrity's family member who pass on. George didn't want an Anna Nicole Smith circus around his brother's death. But the San Antonio media, just as the residents of George's hometown of Pearsall, respect George and his privacy. Ever since George and Norma moved into the Dominion, the San Antonio media has embraced him as a neighbor. Even when he sits court side at the Spurs games, he's left alone.

John Byron "Buddy" Strait was born in Poteet, Texas on May 27, 1950. At the time of his death, Buddy was 59 years old. He had met and married Denise Watkins and together they had three children: Walker Strait, John Byron Strait III and their daughter, Kara Strait Silva who married John Silva. He had three grandchildren by his daughter, Kara, Kailey, Nessa and Avery Silva.

At the time of his death, Buddy's mother was alive down in Georgia in the year of 2009 and his father was still in Pearsall. As stated, George's sister, Pency had married a man by the name of Lea Edel and they had moved to Dallas.

The funeral was held at the Vaughan Funeral Home in Boerne, Texas, just outside San Antonio. Then the body was taken to Pearsall, Texas and a small service was held in the First Baptist Church of Pearsall for those who grew up with the Strait family. After that, Buddy was taken to his final resting place in Big Wells, Texas where a monument was placed adorned by a cowboy's rope. On the front of the tombstone was his name and date of birth and death. On the back, there's a picture of Buddy in his cowboy hat with a passage from the Bible, John 16:22, "Therefore you now have sorrow, but I will see you again, and your heart will rejoice and your joy no one will take from you."

Buddy was like his brother, George. He was a man with a kind heart and a friend to everyone he ever met. He lived a good life, worked hard and loved his family. He spent a good portion of adult life in Alice, Texas for his wife to be near her family's real estate business and he ran his oil field fishing tool business there before he sold out. Ranching took up most of his time after that. He was country, like George. He loved the simple things in life, family, rodeoing and country music. He was a hard worker and lived life to the fullest. He was never jealous of George's success. In fact, a few have said Buddy Strait was just as good a singer as George so Buddy was comfortable with his younger brother's success. Former classmates of Buddy and George's say they were like twins in high school, even though there were two years between them. What one did, the other one did. George followed Buddy in the band before both of them quit to pursue other interests such as roping.

Big Wells, Pearsall and Alice are in a triangle of sorts and any place can be reached within an hour's and a half's drive. It's the oil field where Buddy worked for an oil field company that cements pipe down hole before starting his own company with Jimmy Tymrak. Jan and Jimmy Tymrak and Buddy and Denise Strait became fast friends, personal and in business because like an extended family as the success of the business grew, so did their friendship. If George Strait kept a low profile when he ventured to his ranch in South Texas, Buddy Strait kept an even lower profile than his famous brother. Not a great many of the public knew George had a brother until he died. In South Texas, Buddy and Mr. John Strait lived simple lives like they always had done even after George became famous in 1981. No one ever bothered them such as the media. But there were times when a reporter or two got antsy. Being a simple man with simple needs, Buddy knew how to handle them. A couple of books had been written about George, but there was very little written about Buddy and

Mr. Strait because there wasn't much to tell. Like a cowboy in a Louis L'Amour novel, the Straits were country when country wasn't cool. The Strait's preferred it that way, too. Now it's the rage of the world. Even Prince Phillip has a cowboy hat!

Because Buddy was the man behind the famous man, he could play and sing and rope as good as George without all the hoopla about it. He just never pursued it like George did. He did his thing around the campfires and BBQ pits. In that respect, Buddy and George were as different as night and day. There only common denominator was being family men who loved to rodeo.

Randy Carroll of K-J97 Country Music out of San Antonio went on the air the next morning after Buddy's body was found by that maid at the La Quinta Motor Lodge and asked his listeners to pray for the Strait family and to let them mourn in private. Everyone did just that, their love and respect for George was the key. Oh, there were a few hounds out on the trail because of the autopsy report and the methadone in Buddy's system, but his death was ruled a heart attack, not any kind of drug overdose. Not enough can be said about that because the media would love to find some dirt on the Strait family. Many in the national media couldn't believe that this huge country music star named George Strait had a family as clean as he seemed to be. Clean living doesn't sell a lot of newspapers and magazines. But in the world of country music, scandal is not the norm. Country people like to bask in the success of their comrades. There's scandal alright, but it's usually left up to the divorces rather than the drug induced nightlife of the rock and rollers or movie stars.

In the old days when the peanut crop came in from the fields around Pearsall, farmers would be proud of their neighbor's crop as they did of their own. It's the same way in the country music business. Live clean, work hard and success will come your way. That's the country way of life.

No sooner had George gotten past Buddy's death in April of 2009, his birth mother, Doris Jean Couser Strait Lieber died at the age of 79 on January 30th, 2010.

After Mrs. Lieber left George and Buddy and her husband, John Strait, in the early sixties, she moved to Dallas, Texas with George's sister, Pency. Then George's mother married Paul Malcolm Lieber and moved to Lawrenceville, Georgia. The funeral was held in the Chapel of the Tim Stewart Funeral Home there in Lawrenceville. Lawrenceville, Georgia is known as the location where former Governor George Wallace was shot and paralyzed while running for President in 1968.

Mrs. Lieber was preceded in death by Buddy in 2009 and her husband, Paul Lieber in 1984. There was no mention of Jenifer Strait preceding her in death in Mrs. Lieber's obituary which was strange. The painful past continued to dictate the future for George Strait. The obituary said Mrs. Lieber was survived by Pency Edel of Texas,

George Strait of Texas a step-son from New Jersey named Roy Lieber and a step-daughter named Leslie Neely of Georgia. She was buried beside her husband, Paul. George didn't attend her funeral for reasons of his own. The obituary made no mention of Bubba Strait, her grandson or any of Buddy's family. It didn't mention Norma Strait or Denise Strait. And, it's not known if George or any of the Strait family attended Mrs. Lieber's funeral or graveside service. The funeral home kept it very, very quiet.

George's mother was an art dealer in Georgia where she worked for Alley's Attic. She was a member of Patriot Guard Riders. By all accounts, she got help for her depression and became a loving step-mother and grandmother to the Lieber grandchildren. She didn't attend Jenifer's or Buddy's funerals. The estrangement she instigated long ago in the early 1960's still held true and there was a strain between her and her famous son until her death. In fact, few knew she was George Strait's mother there in Georgia! And she didn't go around Lawrenceville announcing it either. Mrs. Lieber's friends who did know of her past, that she'd once been married to Mr. John B. Strait of Texas and was the mother to the King Of Country Music, well, they kept the secret to themselves as she wished.

But there had to be pain from George at her passing, even though the pain of losing her as a boy of nine had to always be there. When you look at pictures of Doris Lieber and John Strait Sr., one can see which way the looks went.

198

George has Mrs. Lieber's features and Buddy had his daddy's. The younger pictures of Mrs. Strait-Lieber revealed a pretty woman as John Strait was a handsome young man when they lived in Pleasanton, Texas. After the divorce, Mrs. Strait-Lieber found the answers to her depression and then she found a new love in Mr. Paul Lieber who was also divorced. They lived a simple life for a while in Dallas before the move to Georgia. In time, both Doris Strait and John Strait found the happiness they thought they had while married in Texas when they remarried after their divorce.

Three deaths in George Strait's life placed a heavy burden on him. His faith in God and the shoulder of his wife, Norma played the most important part in getting past it all because you never get over it. Losing your only daughter, your beloved brother and the woman who gave you life all in one lifetime would tear anybody apart. But George has always held his head up. He's always had so much going on in his life that keeps him busy to keep his mind off the tragedies that have come his way. With all that George Strait has accomplished, he's lost a lot, too. That's the way life goes for everyone. It's all on how you handle it that makes you the person you are. George had no control over some of the events of his life such as the deaths of his daughter and his brother. But, he has lived on with the happiness his life is today with the successes he's accomplished and the love he receives from his wife and son. He is a huge country music star, probably the biggest in the past 30 years. Maybe one day while sitting on the back porch of his ranch house in deep South Texas, he'll decide to write it all down for his fans, tell how he really feels and how he felt about this and that, especially the painful memories of his losses. No writer can do that for him and no book can tell what was going on in someone's head when the triumphs came and tragedies went by. That's left for George Strait to do if he ever decides to put it all down on paper.

Sixteen
Set Out To Pasture

So what do you do when you've done everything there is in life and acquired all the things you ever wanted out of your life? What do you do when you've lived the good life, endured all the triumphs and tragedies in your life and there's really nothing left to do or anything left to prove? Well, you're set out to pasture to enjoy the fruits of your labor. You'll never have to work again, unless you really want to. You have so much of the wonderful things God has given you and you've become an old war horse needing some time to yourself and take life a little slower. Right? Wrong!

Not George Strait. Oh, there's no doubt he'll stay closer to the pasture, grazing on the green grass of his success. But, he's not done yet! Like an old football player who still has the body to play the game he loves, George still has a few songs left in him, a few head of cattle that need tending and maybe a grand baby to teach the things he was taught by his grandfather, He's got the most supportive wife a man could ever be lucky enough to have, that's for sure.

In the shade of close to 60 years old, George is still making the girls swoon. George's shows are still full of energy and excitement. A typical show in San Antonio's Alamodome in 2007, George and his Ace In The Hole Band left them out of breath and wanting more. The band kicked it off with a great rendition of Bob Wills "Take Me

Back To Tulsa." Then George came on wearing a white shirt, a white hat and a shiny belt buckle from his team roping events. As he holds his Guild guitar, the girls are still going crazy on the front row, some of them half his age! But, George has taken pretty good care of himself. Although there are a few more wrinkles and a few more pounds around the middle section. Laughing at the craziness of it all are George's son, Bubba, his father John with his wife Anna and George's niece, Kara. His shows are so dynamic, it's hard to believe this guy is almost sixty years old. There might not be a pasture that can hold George when he decides to slow it down a bit.

All the hysteria of a George Strait show reminds the audience of those early Beatles shows. Modest to a tee, George will give a quiet "thank you" after each song and maybe a quick bow. His politeness only adds fuel to the fire he has lit in the arena. Retire? Not at the rate George is going.

And he's not stingy with his band. He will let 'em rip and when he stops the show to introduce, you can tell that even though they don't socialize much offstage, on stage they are having a good time as friends and comrades in musical arms.

"I've got this great band, so why not show them off!" George will tell the crowd and they love it. Bob Wills used to do that kind of thing with his Texas Playboys.

In the early part of 2000, George managed to get Bob Wills great fiddle player, Johnny Gimble out of his pasture and play some dates. Gimble had played the Austin City Limits with George and the Ace In The Hole Band back in the mid to late eighties and it was real thrill for George to have Johnny on stage with him. A true legend, Gimble was a rousing member of Wills band right up until the late great country star died. Today, Johnny Gimble lives in Dripping Springs, Texas and is retired. But every once in a blue moon, when the right band calls, the 84 year old Gimble will come out of his own pasture and play some dates.

Backstage, George sometimes rests with a good cigar, usually a Cohiba. He even sang about high-priced stogies in the 1988 hit record "If You Ain't Lovin', You Ain't Livin'" where he sings about smoking them four-bit cigars. He'll drink a beer or two, but he's never been a big drinker. While golfing with his son, Bubba, there'll be a cooler on the golf cart. But, George just takes it easy no matter where he is, golfing or playing concert dates.

For vacations, George and Norma go where ever they want to in the world and have been. In America, George and Norma are regulars at the Kentucky Derby. It's not known if George is a big gambler on the ponies, but he loves a good horse and a good horse race.

There's a lot to say about Norma Strait, even though there's not a lot known about her because that's the way she likes it. And it's all good. Most of it is why George has taken his love on home every night. She's smart, loving and loyal and she has remained beautiful for herself and for her husband. She knows what it takes to please a man and that's why she takes care of herself. If more men and women did that for their spouses, there'd be a lot less divorces. That's not just the sexual part of a marriage. But, honestly, no man or woman wants to come home to a slob or a drunk or a wife beater. Save that for the country songs.

She's weathered the bad times with him and basked in the good ones. She's sown a lot of good seeds to a lot of people she knows and loves. She's worked on her daughter Jenifer's foundation to help people out. She's supported George in everything he's ever done or wanted to do. And, he's supported her. What a novel idea. A couple supporting each other. More couples should try it.

Has it all been peaches and cream? No way! They themselves will tell you that. But they are a team, not unlike that of George and Bubba when they rope together. For almost 40 years, ever since they were nothing but love-struck kids running off to Mexico to get married like they did, they have leaned on each other like God intended. With the divorce rate up to 62% in today's America and the spotlight of super stardom shinning in their faces everyday and riches one can only dream about, George and Norma Strait continue to prove the critics wrong.

So just as Roy and Dale used to wave their hats and ride off into the sunset singing "Happy Trails" to those who loved and supported them, so will George and Norma Strait where they will set out to find their own pasture to spend the rest of their lives. With all that George Strait has done, with all that he's accomplished in his life, all that he's lost, too, he has left his mark on this world. And, like a good gallop on a well-bred horse, George Harvey Strait did it with dignity and respect for everyone he ever encountered.

And, he did all from a little corner of the world called Texas where the sky is big, the wind is a cool breeze, and a land that is truly God's country.

SOME FINAL THOUGHTS

When I started to research and write this book, I hadn't realized how much my life and George Strait's life had run side by side throughout the years. Although I wasn't a personal friend to him, I'd met him on a few occasions. And although I was never to be as rich he became, I had some of the same successes as a writer as George had in music and I made a few bucks here and there. He took playing music to a high I could only dream about and I often did like so many of us who worked those old dance halls back then. But I was a drummer and had no illusions about being anything else. Again, drummers and bass players and guitar pickers are truly a dime a dozen in the music business. It's the star out front that counts.

The one thing that George and I both enjoyed was family and friends and in coming from small South Texas towns, we grew up with a couple of great fathers who always wanted the best for us. And, we both married out of our league, too!

Again, I don't profess to be a personal friend of George Strait, so I don't want the reader to think otherwise. But, I've met him and I know him from those early days when we both played the same clubs, a few times one night apart. That's how a lot of us South Texas musicians knew George Strait and some of the others who have made their mark in the world of entertainment either in music or on the screen. I've been a fan of his entire musical career. I figured that qualified me enough to write this book. Maybe George will write a book of his own one day and really set the record straight.

I don't think anyone can understand George Strait unless they go to South Texas and see why where he came from makes him a private man, only coming out when he's on the stage. The life in South Texas is slower. It begs for you to stop and take a look around at what God has made. That's why George likes to go down there as often as he does, it gets him away from the rat race of the music business. Gives him a place to breathe and sit and think. That's where I grew up, too. When I was researching this book down in Big Wells, Texas, it took me back to a time and place that I love and miss. My father had business in Big Wells in the 1960's in an old onion shed on the edge of town where he parked his oil field trucks for Dow Chemical Company. It's agriculture country. Some 15 miles from Big Wells is the town of Crystal City which is known as the Spinach Capital of Texas with its statue of the cartoon character Popeye.

Whenever a small town boy makes good, there is always a national media outlet that thinks they can get to the heart of the new star by sending one of their nationally know biographers down to dig up the basic information and put out a biography that tells the "real story." In the 1990's, a writer named Jo Sammajo wrote a book on George Strait. In 2001, the nationally known biographer Mark Bego who'd penned many a biographies on the lives of the stars of the world for money wrote a book on

George's life. Both biographies were nothing short of terrible. Now, I hate to say that about a fellow writer, but they weren't there as I was. They'd never met George Strait, his brother or his father. And, they had never played country music, gone to Nashville in the 1970's to try to make it as I had. They had never played those same dance halls as I and George Strait had done. In short, they should try to write about something they know about, which is the first rule of thumb of writing itself. But hey, if the star is bright, take the money and run.

Then, during the research for this book, seeing the old Wishing Well Club in Pearsall, Texas where I played and where George played, well, it just brought back so many memories.

And, the people! Because life is slower, they seem to be friendlier down there. George's father reminded me of my father. He was kind as we talked about his sons freely because he took the time to visit and so did I. I don't think we stop and visit in the city like we do in the country. When Ron Kattner brought me the picture of the old Cheatham Street Warehouse where George really got his start and where I played for dances there in the early 70's, well, it just brought back my childhood, my teenage years, drinking cold beer and chasing Southwest Texas State University coeds. I guess that's another reason George goes back to those small towns from time to time, to reflect and to remember. (But I don't think he chased SWTSU coeds, however.)

I hope the reader will take the time to go on down to South Texas to see what Texas really is like. Dallas is not Texas nor is Houston, in my opinion. They're great cities, but they're just too many people to truly be Texas.

And stop at one of those old wooden dance halls where they still throw corn meal on the wooden floor for you to really kick up your heels. Halls like the old Wagon Wheel in Jourdanton, the old Kicker Palace in Poteet or halls like Sengelmann Hall in Schulenburg or Schroeder Hall near Goliad, Texas, or Sun Valley in Victoria or Dalton's Beer Joint in Pleasanton, Texas. I know you'll feel the authentic beat of a good honky-tonk band and drink some ice cold beer and look over the nice, pretty Texas women. Man, there's nothing like it in the world! When the perfume and the after shave lotion mix with a hot summer night and the beer flows cold accented by a solid country beat from a swinging country band, there's Heaven right here on Earth!

I hope you enjoyed getting to know George Strait a little better as much as I did. In working on this book, I learned a lot about him, too. You know, when you meet someone, you never know they are going to be rich and famous. When I was at the University of Arkansas, a law professor at a fraternity party I attended wore a beard and was standing by the keg. He introduced himself to me. "Hi, I'm Bill Clinton." Wow! Never thought he would move on to be a two-term President Of The United States, but he did. And, when I shook George Strait's hand the first time at that talent show in Cotulla, Texas when we we're both in the FFA, I had no idea he'd become the King Of Country Music, but he did and he remains the King today.

So if you're ever in South Texas, stop and take a look around at that part of the world. It was our little corner of the world, mine and George Strait's and everyone we ever knew when we were growing up. We all share that beginning no matter where we ended up or what we ended up doing. Famous or not, South Texas will treat everyone the same. That's the way George Strait likes it. So do I. And there really is no finer place to be from. It truly is Heaven right here on this Earth.

Special Note: Linda Robbins has put together a website called "StraitFever.com" and it is simply wonderful. She's not a director of the Foundation or even a member of the Strait family, she's just a dedicated fan who took the time to put together one of the best websites I've ever seen. Go to it! And, if you'd like to donate to The Jenifer Strait Foundation, make a check payable to:

The Jenifer Strait Foundation

And send it to:
Dilley State Bank
The Jenifer Strait Memorial Foundation
c/o Jeff Avant, President
P.O. Box 9
Dilley, Texas 78017-0009

I'm sure George, Norma and Bubba would appreciate it and the kids you'll be helping will thank you, too.

DISCOGRAPHY

Main Albums:

1. Strait Country (1981)
2. Strait From The Heart (1982)
3. Right Or Wrong (1983)
4. Does Ft. Worth Ever Cross Your Mind (1984)
5. Something Special (1985)
6. #7 (1986)
7. Ocean Front Property (1987)
8. If You Ain't Lovin' You Ain't Livin' (1988)
9. Beyond The Blue Moon Neon (1989)
10. Livin' It Up (1990)
11. Chill Of An Early Fall (1991)
12. Holding My Own (1992)
13. Easy Come, Easy Go (1993)
14. Lead On (1994)
15. Blue Clear Sky (1996)
16. Carrying Your Love With Me (1997)
17. One Step At A Time (1998)
18. Always Never The Same (1999)
19. George Strait (2000)
20. The Road Less Traveled (2001)
21. Honkytonkville (2003)
22. Somewhere Down In Texas (2005)
23. In Just Comes Natural (2006)
24. Troubadour (2008)
25. Twang (2009)

Note: George has also sung duets with Frank Sinatra, Alan Jackson and Patty Loveless and had a Christmas Album out, too.

FILMS/TELEVISION

Movie/Television	Year	Role
The Soldier w/Ace In The Hole Band	1982	Himself
Pure Country Chandler	1992	Dusty Wyatt
Horse Whisperer Soundtrack Only	1998	
Grand Champion	2002	Himself
King Of The Hill Of Cornell	2003	Voice

Note: The sequel to the 1992 movie Pure Country is titled " Pure Country 2: The Gift" was released in a limited run in October of 2010. George did a cameo in the movie and decided not to repeat his role as Dusty Chandler. In truth, George is slowing down quite a bit now days. He prefers to spend his down time from the tour with his wife and son. And he values the time with his dad down in Pearsall and Big Wells as Mr. Strait is getting on up there himself in age.

AWARDS
Organization / Award

1. **1985 Academy of Country Music**
    Top Male Vocalist
2. **1985 Country Music Association**
    Male Vocalist of the Year
3. **l985 Country Music Association**
    Album of the Year
4. **1985 Academy Of Country Music**
    Top Male Vocalist
5. **1986 Music City News Country**
    Male Artist of the Year
6. **1986 Country Music Association**
    Male Vocalist of the Year
7. **1986 Billboard**
    Top Country Artist
8. **1987 Billboard**
    Top Country Artist
9. **1988 Academy Of Country Music**
    Top Male Vocalist
10. **1989 Country Music Association**
    Entertainer of the Year
11. **1989 Special Award**
    Connnie B. Gay Award
12. **1989 Academy Of Country Music**
    Entertainer of the Year
13. **1989 Special Award**
    Presidential American
14. **1990 Country Music Association**
    Entertainer of the Year
15. **1990 Radio & Records**
    Country Performer of
16. **1991 American Music Awards**
    Favorite Country Male
17. **1993 ACM**
    Tex Ritter Movie of the
18. **1995 Academy Of Country Music**
    Single of the Year

19. 1995 ASCAP
    Voice Of Music Award
20. 1996 TNN/Music City News
    Video of the Year
21. 1996 TNN/Music City News
    Single of the Year
22. 1996 TNN/Music City News
    Album of the Year
23. 1996 Country Music Association
    Single of the Year
24. 1996 Radio & Records
    Best Male Vocalist
25. 1996 Radio & Records
    Best Single
26. 1996 Radio & Records
    Most Valuable Performers
27. 1996 Billboard
    Top Country Artist
28. 1997 TNN/Music City News
    Album of the Year
29. 1997 Country Music Association
    Male Vocalist of the Year
30. 1997 Country Music Association
    Album of the Year
31. 1997 American Music Awards
    Favorite Country Album
32. 1997 Academy Of Country Music
    Top Male Vocalist
33. 1997 Academy Of Country Music
    Album of the Year
34. 1997 Radio & Records
    Best Album For Blue
35. 1997 Radio & Records
    Best Male Vocalist
36. 1996 Billboard
    Most Played Artist
37. 1998 Country Music Association
    Male Vocalist of the Year

38. 1998 American Music Awards
    Favorite Country Male
39. 1998 American Music Awards
    Favorite Country Album
40. 1998 Radio & Records
    Best Male Vocalist
41. 1999 Country Weekly Golden Pick
    Awards - Favorite Line Dance
42. 1999 Country Weekly Golden Pick
    Awards - Favorite Video
43. 1999 Country Weekly Golden Pick
    Awards - Favorite Male Artist
44. 1999 Country Weekly Golden Pick
    Awards - Favorite Entertainer
45. 1999 Country Weekly/TNN/CMT Music
    Album of the Year
46. 2000 Country Weekly/TNN/CMT Music
    Impact Artist of the Year
47. 2000 Country Weekly/TNN/CMT Music
    Single of the Year
48. 2000 Country Weekly/TNN/CMT Music
    Male Artist of the Year
49. 2000 Country Weekly/TNN/CMT Music
    Entertainer of the Year
50. 2000 Country Weekly/TNN/CMT Music
    Album of the Year
51. 2000 Country Music Association
    Vocal Event of the Year
52. 2001 Country Music Association
    Song of the Year
53. 2007 Country Music Association
    Album of the Year
54. 2008 Country Music Association
    Single of the Year
55. 2008 Country Music Association
    Album of the Year
56. 2009 Grammy Awards
    Best Country Album

57. 2009 Academy Of Country Music Artist of the Decade

Worth Noting: As of October of 2010, George Strait holds the record for the most number one hit records of any musical genre. To achieve this is like pitching 8 no hitters in baseball or winning 8 Super Bowls. Can it be broken? Sure it can, but not anytime soon.

PROFESSIONAL RODEO COWBOY
ASSOCIATION OF AMERICA
(PRCA) EVENTS

George Strait sponsors the George Strait Team Roping Event at the Prairie Rose in San Antonio, Texas and has for the past 28 years when he and his brother, Buddy started it in Kingsville, Texas in 1982. He has been a professional rodeo rider for most of his life as is his son, Bubba who is 28 years old this year. Team roping is their chosen event and they've won many times over the past 10 years. Both learned to ride at an early age as roping and riding is in their blood.

Although George and his son, Bubba have slowed down on roping, they still sponsor the George Strait Team Roping Classic in San Antonio. Since George has so little time to spare, he takes in a PRCA Event whenever he can. But, it's his Roping Classic that he makes sure he's there to see it's done right.

In March of 2010, the event was a sellout. Actor James Pickens. Jr. best known as Chief Richard Webber on the ABC series "Grey's Anatomy" is a true team roping fan and showed up at the 28th Annual GSTRC to try to get some pointers from George on how to run a successful event like his. The gracious actor, who is also a board member of the PRCA, met with George after the event to try to pick his brain for ideas about an event that Pickens wants to start in California. A California Cowboy? Didn't know one existed! The actor was very thankful for the ideas and met with fans, taking time for photos, including pictures with George's niece, Kara

Strait Silva and George's Fan Club President, Anita O'Brian.

The dates for the roping event for next year, 2011 are set for March 11th and 12th at the same location, The Rose Palace. Tickets went on sale on October 4th and are $20 bucks for each day. But, there probably won't be any left after November.

The 2010 event saw header Jake Long and heeler Coleman Proctor win the Grand Prize out of 468 other teams. These boys have been best friends since they were toddlers. After two days of intense competition, the dust settled and they were declared the winners. They finished with a 14.93 combined time and rode away with two custom painted George Strait Team Roping Classic Championship Chevy Silverado Trucks from Cavendar Chevrolet out of Boerne, Texas. They also won two Strait X-treme horse trailers from Bruton Trailers, two Twister saddles from Tractor Supply, Resistol roping bags, jackets from Wrangler and Justin, Gist belt buckles and half of the $159,630 cash payoff. That's some serious winnings.

Each year the event is sponsored by HEB, the large food store based in Texas with stores in Mexico, Justin Boots, Tractor Supply, Frost Bank of San Antonio, Capital Farm Credit, Wrangler, Hill Country Tractor, Gist Belt Buckles, Bill Miller BBQ and Resistol. Flashy Texas lawyer Wayne Wright also puts up some of that car wreck money he gets in the courthouses of Texas as a sponsor.

Texans love their rodeos. The largest in the world are in Texas, Houston and San Antonio being the most famous along with the one in Ft. Worth. Almost every small town has a Stock Show and Rodeo of its own with the FFA Chapters and the 4-H Chapters showing farm animals for ribbons and trophies.

Legend has it that the PRCA was formed by a group of cowboys in Deer Trail, Colorado on July 4, 1869 to settle an argument over who was the best at performing everyday ranching tasks. That competition is considered to be the first rodeo which evolved into rodeo as we know it today.

Today's professional rodeo cowboy is a bit different from his 1800's predecessor, but the ideals and showmanship and hard work are still valued by today's competitors. A cowboy's standing in the rodeo community is still dependent on his skill with the rope or his ability to ride a bucking animal. The cowboy code still dictates that a cowboy ought to help his fellow competitors, even though they might be competing for the same prize or paycheck. That is still the basis of George Strait's Team Roping Event every year.

While some things have changed since those days gone by, most of the changes have been for the better and to make things safer for the competitors in the events of a rodeo where danger is always just around the corner.

Now the cowboy travels much of the time in custom-made rigs or flies from one rodeo to another. Marketing and business acumen have become as crucial as roping, wrestling or riding skills. If you plan to make a living at it, you'd better do both equally well. Cowboys are competing for more money than ever now days. Rodeos are even on cable T.V. night and day.

Even if a PRCA member doesn't have the inclination to spend more than 200 days a year on the road in search of a berth in the Wrangler National Finals Rodeo, the sport's Super Bowl, he can participate in one of many rodeos close to home each year. Over 600 are held throughout the country year 'round, from small towns to Las Vegas, Nevada.

The Professional Rodeo Cowboy Association was created almost by accident in 1936 when a group of cowboys walked out of a rodeo in the Boston Gardens to protest the actions of rodeo promoter W.T. Johnson who refused to add to the cowboys' entry fees to the rodeo's total purse. Johnson finally gave in to the cowboys' demands and the successful "strike" led to the formation of the Cowboys' Turtle Association.

The cowboys chose that name because, while they were slow to organize, when push came to shove, they weren't afraid to stick their necks out to get what they wanted. In 1945, the Turtles changed their name to the Rodeo Cowboys Association and in 1975, they became the PRCA.

The PRCA staff consists of about 70 full-time employees, but grows to nearly 100 during the peak rodeo season. The PRCA headquarters, established in 1979, is in Colorado Springs, Colorado and also houses the Pro Rodeo Hall Of Fame and Museum of the American Cowboy.

Finally, the creed of the PRCA is to establish the rich traditions and values that are the cornerstone of the cowboy way and to experience the love of animals, completion, excitement and the western lifestyle. The PRCA is established as the global leaders in producing superior rodeo events, products and services by developing innovations that pay tribute to one of the oldest sports in America.

WHAT THE STARS SAY

"I've known George Strait for many years and it has been my pleasure to see his career go straight, no pun intended, up to the rank of superstar. He is a hard working and caring person, a great country music singer, a good actor, a great guy and fellow Texan."

---George Jones

"I've been a big George Strait fan ever since I heard "Unwound" on the radio in Charlotte, North Carolina. I also sang a lot of his music in the clubs through the seventies and early eighties."

---Randy Travis

"I am doing what I am doing today because of the Good Lord, my family and George Strait."

---Garth Brooks

"One person whose career I've always admired and his music, too, is George Strait. He just keeps coming out with great music."

---Alan Jackson

"George will always go down in my book as one of the great vocalists and great entertainers in our business."

---John Anderson

"His voice is just so rich and powerful, yet beautiful. When he sings a song, that sucker's going to number one. We've got all of his albums at our house, and we love listening to them all."

---Billy Ray Cyrus

"He's my biggest idol. George is a nice, nice man and I've gotten to sing with him a couple of times. I love his music, always have."

---John Michael Montgomery

"I've competed with a lot of different people, but I have my special people that I love to compete with. George and I have always competed. I love him, but I love to compete, too."

---Reba McEntire

"I buy all his albums, everything he puts out. That's the kind of career I want, like George Strait."

---Tracy Byrd

"George Strait's body of work will stand the test of time as well as Hank Williams, George Jones or anybody else. I admire George Strait a lot for his consistency and the earthiness he brings to the table."

---Marty Stuart

WHAT THE CRITICS SAY

"It's too easy to suggest that George Strait has profited tremendously from his clean-cut good looks and his sensitive Hank image. He really hasn't cut a bad record. Therein lies the secret of his success."

---David McGee

Rolling Stone Album Guide

"It takes time for even the most gifted musicians to mature and everything about George Strait's performances from his skilled vocals to the tasteful, elaborate production values was a tangible notch above."

---Randy Lewis

Los Angeles Times

"Sometimes you wonder: Is country music getting worse or is Strait just getting better and better?"

---David Zimmerman

USA Today

"In 30 years, George Strait has scarcely cut a song without some redeeming quality, much less released a whole album of them, which is why his career has come to resemble Nashville's answer to the Energizer Bunny: He just keeps on going while others fall by the wayside."

----Rick Mitchell

Houston Chronicle

"George Strait isn't a phony, and that isn't a faint praise. Those who still look to country for the simple things treasure the matter-of-fact of the man who could have been named by a press agent, but wasn't."

---Robert Christgau

Christgau's Record Guide

"George Strait continues to get better and better. Partly, it's the maturity of his voice and the authority that it carries. It's also the songs. It's unlikely that there's anyone in the country with a better ear for songs."

---Chet Flippo

Billboard

"George Strait's voice is as familiar and welcomed as a comfortable pair of Wranglers and broken-in Justin boots."

---Mario Tarradell

Country: The Essential Album Guide

ACKNOWLEDGEMENTS

When you write a book of any kind, there is always someone else who helped make it happen...and here they are!

Ron Kattner and John Berlet, the men behind the curtain. Linda Robbins of *straitfever.com,* the lady with a lot of the pictures in the book. She is the consummate George Strait fan. (Please visit her website for a great ride!) Banning Lary, my harshest critic. I think old Banning actually hates me, but he keeps taking my calls for help. Jeff Edwards, the smartest man with the best plan. Jeff knows business and he knows publishing through his company InterSkillMedia of Austin, Texas. T.J. and Sandra Greaney of Country Line Magazine in Austin, Texas. They have a very good read for the true country music fan. Country Weekly Magazine, THE COUNTRY MUSIC MAGAZINE OF AMERICA, The Nashville Tennessean, the news of Tennessee KASE and KVET radio in Austin, Texas. The Pleasanton Express in Pleasanton, Texas, home of the cowboy. The Frio Nueces Current in Pearsall, Texas, a pretty good little newspaper. The staff of the Pearsall High School who actually got up from behind their desks and dug up information without any problems whatsoever, especially Mary Benavides. The Poteet Chamber of Commerce, The Pearsall Chamber of Commerce Johnny Bush for just being Johnny Bush. (I've got to be his biggest fan and have shared a stage with him off and on over the past 38 years. George Strait is a true fan, too.) Gary Teutsch, my brother who always takes my calls, too. Jason and Holly and Tim at the Manchaca road branch of the Austin Public Library for all their help. The library is the BEST place to write a book. It even has a bathroom and air conditioning and there's no office rent! Randy Phillips, Judy Crabb, Helen Alexander, Jamie Brown (Man of Sound) Martine Chavarria, David Gilliland,Terry Fields and Dawn and E.W. Jansen. These are true friends I can always count on. Eddie Trevino, Lalo Trevino and Diana Hernandez, classmates of George Strait's at Pearsall High School who went out of their way to add something to this book. Diana even broke out all her class pictures from Pearsall High School annuals for me to look over and choose. And Mr. John Byron Strait, Sr. for the ride in his new truck and the information he gave me. A truly nice man. Darn it, I almost forgot Jimmy Tymrak, Buddy Strait's business partner and a former Jourdanton High School classmate of mine. Salt of the Earth, a true Texan.

Oh, and my Mom and my Dad.

And last but not least, my sons, Taylor and Parker Teutsch. A love without end, amen!

Thanks for that one, George!

ABOUT THE AUTHOR

Austin Teutsch grew up just down the road from George Strait in Jourdanton, Texas where he graduated from Jourdanton High School in 1973. He promptly entered the University of Arkansas in Fayetteville, Arkansas. He has been playing country music since he was 14 years old, slipping in the back doors of some of the roughest honky-tonks and roadhouses in Texas to chase a dream of his own. (Ever play the Red Dog Lounge in Freer, Texas?)

He came back to Texas in 1980 and married in 1981. Over the next 25 years, Mr. Teutsch had two wonderful sons, Taylor 19 and Parker 14, two best selling biographies on the lives of Wal-Mart founder Sam Walton and former Texas Congresswoman Barbara Jordan and many articles in publications around the country.

He has worked on the biographies of Dick York of *"Bewitched"* fame and Jimmy Nicol, a drummer who actually *played* as a Beatle when Ringo Starr was in the hospital in 1964.

Austin Teutsch has lived in Austin, Texas for 27 years and is, unfortunately, single.

Send him an e-mail at austinteutsch@aol.com if you like the book. (Or even if you don't like the book) He'd like to hear from you.

ALSO BY AUSTIN TEUTSCH

THE SAM WALTON STORY

BARBARA JORDAN: THE BIOGRAPHY

SHANKED!
THE RUSSELL ERXLEBEN STORY

AN ARMY OF IDIOTS*
* Fiction

TO ORDER MORE COPIES OF:

KING GEORGE

The Triumphs And Tragedies
In The Life Of George Strait

THE KING OF COUNTRY MUSIC

please visit

www.StraitBook.com

Made in the USA
Lexington, KY
16 December 2010